THIS BOOK BELONGS TO _____

sign after
the X _____

MARINA ROY

ADVANCE | ARTSPEAK
Vancouver

SIGN AFTER THE X
Copyright © 2001 by Marina Roy

All rights reserved. No part of this book may be reproduced or used in any form by any means – graphic, electronic or mechanical – without the prior written permission of the publisher, except by a reviewer, who may use brief excerpts in a review, or in the case of photocopying, a license from the Canadian Copyright Licensing Agency.

ADVANCE EDITIONS
an imprint of
ARSENAL PULP PRESS
103-1014 HOMER STREET
VANCOUVER, BC
CANADA V6B 2W9
arsenalpulp.com

ARTSPEAK
an artist run centre

233 CARRALL STREET
VANCOUVER, BC
CANADA V6B 2J2
artspeak.bc.ca

Arsenal Pulp Press gratefully acknowledges the support of the Canada Council for the Arts and the British Columbia Arts Council for its publishing program, and the Government of Canada through the Book Publishing Industry Development Program for its publishing activities.

Artspeak is a member of the Pacific Association of Artist Run Centres (PAARC). Artspeak gratefully acknowledges the support of the Canada Council for the Arts, the Government of British Columbia through the BC Arts Council, the City of Vancouver, the Vancouver Foundation, The BC Gaming Commission, Heritage Canada, our volunteers and members.

Book design by Dean Allen and Solo
Illustrations, unless otherwise noted, by Marina Roy
Printed and bound in Canada

CANADIAN CATALOGUING IN PUBLICATION DATA:
Roy, Marina.
     Sign after the x

     Copublished by: Artspeak Gallery
     ISBN 1-55152-112-1

     1. X (The letter). 2. Signs and symbols—Social aspects. I. Artspeak Gallery. II. Title.
     P211.7.R69 2001   302.2'223   C2001-911278-5

For G.

$x^0 = 1$ whatever x is: even when $x = 0$, $0^0 = 1$.

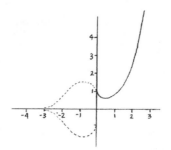

f(x) = x^x

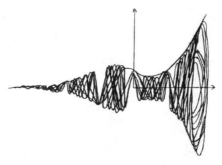

x^x spindle

(somewhere on the horizon)
appears zero
then one
and variations on the theme
the ego
and you over there

(what can you do for me?
what can I do for you?)

now dig a hole
and put me in it
mark it x

back to square one
and zero again
and variations on the theme

contents

illustrations, tables, graphs, & maps

foreword

The writer has broken down language into one of its elementary components, a particular letter, or grapheme, and has mapped out an itinerary for this letter, with multiple entrances, connections, divergences, dead ends. The reader can easily pick up the thread here, or there, create their own itinerary, add new paths, go well beyond the scope of this book. This is not a genealogy. More a sustained language game that multiple players can play. Beyond the restrictions of time and space.

It so happens that this letter has the smallest entry for words beginning with it in the dictionary. Its use as a first letter is limited to words of Greek origin mostly, or to those of African, Chinese, Vietnamese, or North/Central/ South American native origin. It encompasses the discourse of that so-called "other," filling in for a variety of velars, fricatives or sibilants, but also for those sounds that our "Indo-European" tongue can't quite grasp. Within prefixes and suffixes in the English language (such as *ex-, -ex, -ax, -ox, -ix, -ux*), this letter abounds. X is ubiquitous in Latin, proliferating in the many inflected versions of its words (*rex, lex, dixit*, etc.). The letter as an isolated grapheme has always been used in scientific and philosophical discourses to stand in for an unknown or variable quantity, measurement, or quality. $y=x$.

It approaches the end, but never quite reaches it. It is not even penultimate, but antepenultimate (x,y,z). It is always belated. Short of the mark. Like Zeno's paradox, the arrow never quite reaches its final destination. Not a vicious cycle, just constantly degrading (or building itself up again in another form). One is always only half way to the mark. As in carbon dating. Something, a movement in space, can never reach ground zero. This letter or symbol is therefore also about the impossibility of a beginning or an end, the origin and the apocalypse. The endless series of preliminary and end matter, the superstructure of the book, echoes this impossibility: "Things fall apart...."

It is often placed in a marginal position compared to other letters. Exoticized, as it were. A stranger to its own language. There is excitement in its pronunciation, not to mention the seductive quality it lends to the context of the word, as with words like maximum, sexual, parallax. It retains all connotations of speed and dynamism in such words as extreme, axis, flux. This is no accident. The diagonal movement of its sound seems to imitate the articulation, from the long movement of air through a closed larynx, to the closing of the back of the mouth, to the hissing or vibrating of breath through teeth. The oral stimulation of pronunciation is at once pleasurable and challenging. Tension and release.

Twentieth-century semiotics states that the sign, even the grapheme, has an arbitrary relationship to meaning, representation, or, sound: it is based on convention. But it could be argued that all graphemes have the radical double function of ideogram and phoneme. That is, at their root, letters were based on graphic representation as well as pronunciation. Image, meaning, and sound in one. This book approaches this idea on many levels. X has appeared on cave walls as one of the first symbols of language/representation/symbolism. It conveys a certain life force (and death force) unto itself, as our contemporary culture has evinced in the past half century or so. The discourse of otherness (xeno), youth culture (Generation X), UFOS (*X-Files*), comix (*X-Men*), sexuality, genetics, and cyberculture.

Seen from above, x is an island made into a labyrinthine city. A utopian construction that lies unfinished and in ruins out in the middle of an ocean.

Knowledge is only as advanced as a language has evolved. New specialized scientific languages are being created that the "average" person will never know. In this respect, the modernist project is alive and well. Computer languages, for example, they make themselves, create themselves into existence, decide what structure human thought will take, as systems of knowledge have always done. What we do not know, what we cannot know, because of the limits of our language, is known as x. It is in the realm of the transcendent, the underworld, the sublime. It stands in for what is imminent but overlooked or repressed (the Real). X approaches the muteness of the world again. But it is never neutral.

We give names to things. Only those things that are named can be known, possessed. Those we cannot name preside over us. The general system is found hidden within the letter's very configuration. The beauty of the letter is that it is always coming and going, being remembered and forgotten, passing away, and taking on new forms.

Table 1 This table of relative frequencies is based on passages taken from newspapers and novels, and the total sample was 100,362 alphabetic characters. The table was compiled by H. Beker and F. Piper, and originally published in *Cipher Systems: The Protection Of Communication*.

Letter	Percentage	Letter	Percentage
a	8.2	n	6.7
b	1.5	o	7.5
c	2.8	p	1.9
d	4.3	q	0.1
e	12.7	r	6.0
f	2.2	s	6.3
g	2.0	t	9.1
h	6.1	u	2.8
i	7.0	v	1.0
j	0.2	w	2.4
k	0.8	x	0.2
l	4.0	y	2.0
m	2.4	z	0.1

prologue

"From the moment that the circle turns, that the book is wound
back upon itself, that the book repeats itself, its self-identity
receives an imperceptible difference which allows us to step effec-
tively, rigorously, and thus discreetly, out of the closure. Redou-
bling the closure, one splits it. Then one escapes it furtively,
between two passages through the same book, through the same
line, following the same bend…. This departure outside of the
identical within the same remains very slight, it weighs nothing, it
thinks and weighs the book as such. The return to the book is also
the abandoning of the book." [1]

abcd….

*The ox tilled the soil day after day, from sun up to sun down. He often
thought about what it would be like to be free, unyoked from the endless
stretch of soil, from the gaze of the blazing sun, from the back and forth of
one's nose to the soil, like the painstaking drudgery of poring over indecipherable chicken-scratch.*

Always back to square one.

*His mind would often turn to the dream of a pre-fettered existence,
of the watering hole, before the burden of fire, the hammering of form-
lessness into tool. An empty, suffering, heaving articulation of meat and
bone. Caught in a name. A function. A property. A pecking order.*

A monosyllabic vowel and consonant. A truth and a lie, a negation and a knot. Without accent. Gruff and terse. Sliced off from….

Most of the time, he'd turn it off. A numbness was better than the aches and pains. If only these buggering bastards could understand. Stop swearing and sweating and spitting and screwing. Too many mouths to feed and not enough to go 'round. And he, forsaken. For fuck's sake…. Bound to the upside-down A of the plough. "I am your beginning, your sustenance, an improvement on your measly arms and legs, and yet you sentence me to the status of supreme shit."

...

The family stayed home. A half sack. Tic-tac-toe and broken record blue-grass in the background. The ox slept noisily in the barn. Heaving and huffing and puffing after an evening meal of hay. Dry, dry, dry, dry, dry, and then a splash of dirty water.

It couldn't go on. And yet it did. Over and over, one by one by one, until finally, each croaked. Voices fading off. And silence for a while. But then there would be a new one that came along, and kept him from being loose. Home on the range. Hope followed by disappointment, inter-spersed with monotony.

He got bitter over the centuries and in time a new dream came to replace the original one. Or a scheme, rather. A possible vignette:

A burning house / a smoldering field. Put a curse on the homestead. Drive them to drink by making their lives too easy for them. Sloth to pig to lemming. And then finally freedom.

...

One night, one not so different from other nights. TV flickering cyan. Fallen asleep. Drowned in a doze of 26 oz. Bottle empty. Knocked over. The Camel cigarette, loosely saddled between index and middle fingers, burning down and down, flame creeping slowly over humps of tobacco, gently down the tube, into the sunset, slowly dying out. Except for one little twinkling in the distance. A spark is spared, catching a single synthetic fiber of shag. Flickering gently as if on the tip of a scintillating needle. Smoke begins to engulf all the fag burns marking the sea of scum-stained carpet. This burn would last forever, become his oasis, a huge charcoal construction of bodies baking in the sun.

There is always the fear, the doubt, that upon getting closer, as so many times in the past, it would all disappear, his hopes, his dreams, as if never there to begin with.

...

At the end of the journey, there was a return to the delta, the door of his birth. The Nile, the Euphrates, the St. Lawrence, the Mississippi, the Neva, the Fraser, the Amazon, the Tigris. The route back, unremarkable, strangely commonplace, much like the discovery of a buried dream. The familiarity of milk. Layers of silt, smell of salt. Sniffing out the territory as you make your way upstream. A sense of giving in. A couple of coins thrown in the right direction only lessens the burden. After the pyramid of progress is the equilateral of descent. All hope hinging on how many bottles you leave at the doorstep. Seems to take forever to get there....

Ox: an adult castrated bull of the genus *Bos*. (See Appendix C)

Cattle [Middle English *catel*, personal property, livestock, from Old North French, from Medieval Latin *capitale*, property, from Latin, neuter of *capitalis*, chief, primary, from *caput*, head. Indo-European root **kaput**].

boustrophedon: *n*. An ancient method of writing in which the lines are inscribed alternately from right to left and from left to right. [Greek *boustrophedon*, turning like an ox (while ploughing): *bous*, ox + *strephein*, to turn]. [2]

"In hieroglyphic and hieratic, an ox-head 𐤀 was a determinative defining the sort of meat to be used in rituals like funerary offerings, but for Semitic speakers it could be made to stand for its initial letter in Semitic, the glottal stop which is sometimes described as a 'coughed ah', or the sound Cockney (or 'estuary English' as it has become) pronounces for the tt in 'bottle'. Later, it would change its pronunciation again, becoming our letter a, with numerous pronunciations, depending on language and context. This is the reverse of our alphabet-book rhymes: A is for 'archer.' In effect, our scribe specifies: 'Ox' (𐤀 /alep) stands for the initial glottal stop, which will later become our a." [3]

introduction

A fog, perhaps on the point of lifting, looms at the crossroads. You've already been waiting for what seems like forever. Or maybe having arrived too late, you stand there like an idiot. What could well be a missed encounter. A long time to wait when there's nothing to see, not knowing if the waiting's for nought. You've been on the road for days. Trucks lifting up clouds of dust as they roar past. And constantly wondering about this meeting all the while. A possible hoax. But all steps have been traced back to here. The supposed scene of the crime.

Spatially, the fog absorbs you. Overnight was sleepless, buried in pitch black. Now that dawn is about to break, it is disorientating, flattening. You think of blindness. The obscurity transports you to imagined spaces that stand in for an already forgotten one. Where the sun has already been shining, high in the sky. Somewhere east where the day is just about done, already immersed in a dark felt blanket.

Every so often, out of the push and pull of cloud, emerge flashes of a hidden world, shadowy blobs, pine tops, the trajectory of trunkless legs, the descent of a stone tower, the teeter-totter of crows, a TV aerial raking the thick grey sky. You wonder if you have been hallucinating from exhaustion or from lack of sleep.

But as you witness this fleeting, fragmented landscape, what seems like an invisible hand begins to sketch in the outlines of an overlapping universe. Uncannily suggestive at first, then ever more familiar as the sketch proceeds from fore to background. And then suddenly,

as if out of nowhere, a luminosity pierces the whole mess of competing lines, erasing them all in one fell swoop. A Turner. Like being help-
lessly suspended in a jar of cloudy piss.

Floating, you proceed to relieve yourself right then and there. Wet-
ting yourself in the beauty of the moment. Lost to the world. You
mark a spot. A point well worn, now your own. To be dispersed in
all directions. A current to light up the world. Your eyes come to rest
in and around the puddle forming between your feet. A hapless ant
burdened by a crumb, the odd stone glistening, tiny shards of mirror
and orange taillight, a greasy plastic bag. You clean your eye glasses.

Turning your gaze upwards from the dirt, a vanishing point begins
to take on dimension. But you are never quite sure whether this is real
or an illusion. A visible line between earth and sky and an infinitesi-
mal point where the road dematerializes. You turn to the other three
directions. The same phenomenon. To the east, a speck has begun to
take on form. Like a black fly making a beeline right for your eye. As
it gets closer you are struck by the familiarity of the silhouette, the
stumbling gait. Finally, it is *I*.

I looks a little drawn. You ask no questions. You and *I* walk west-
ward. *I* with the map. You with the shovel. It has been ten years since
it was buried. With the money. And all looks different now. Trees have
been cut down, roads paved, houses put up, lakes made. The cross-
road is now an intersection. The map is useless. Still, *I* looks for a clue
in the landscape that would solve the many riddles of the map. One
thousand three hundred and thirteen paces west from the intersection, then one hundred and sixty-six due north. Thirteen paces from
a large boulder. We are supposed to be in a forest at this point. There
is no boulder. The forest is non-existent except for one lone tree. The
journey ends there. If the compass does not lie, the case should lie
about four feet underground. With the body. You and I proceed to
dig.

preface

Idle reader, I must warn you that this book is far from complete. In many respects it may seem to lack any centre or purpose. It is riddled with lacunae. It is crazed and fragmented. A dispersal of random, arbitrary facts. Many of the judgments may appear false, facts askew and fabricated in accordance with some ideology or irrational structure. Decomposition. Accumulation of symptoms. Excavation of forgotten histories. Most cultural and linguistic investments in the letter x carry the grain of something inherently fatal.

On first perusing this book you may think that it is an attempt to relay an exhaustive account of x. In fact, this book is divided into two parts. All that has been written here and all that has not. In writing this, I have constructed a limit to thought. In reading, one tests the soundness of that limit, circling it, performing a ritual trespassing of that boundary. Back and forth. Testing out the alien waters lying just beyond.

In 1969, Georges Perec wrote a metatextual book called *La disparition*. A lipogram (from the Greek, *lipogrammaros*, wanting a letter) is constructed from every single letter of the alphabet but "e," the most frequently occurring letter in most "Indo-European" languages. Clearly quite a feat. But the forfeiting of this letter from one's vocabulary carries with it a price. The absence is too absurd, becomes alienating, a pretext. This handicap drains any "soul" out of the language. In the very absence of this essential element, the forcedness and compromising quality of the language begins to speak of extinction, emptiness, and loss of meaning. A possible comment on the "state of things" as it were. *Sign after the X* approaches language in perhaps a diametrically opposed manner – to construct a book using one of the least used letters, especially in terms of words beginning with it. In dissecting this letter one attempts to uncover meaning behind that which is used to express what is knowable and unknowable. Sometimes the unknowable becomes rationalized and instituted as natural and knowable. For instance with Law (*leg-* : to gather; to speak; law; language [*logos*]).

This book will disappoint anyone looking for rigorous research, a distinct category, or a fully developed subject. It is bricolage and the limits are x. This may seem arbitrary to some. But when one realizes that x also stands in for all that lies beyond the threshold of what is knowable, a pattern begins to emerge. This book finds its meaning at the point of intersection between all x-related terms within the realm of written and unwritten law.

But enough. Without further ado, I offer you, kind reader, the fruits of my whimsical and half-assed labour.

translator's note

The following quotation describes the "origin" of the letter x as grapheme and phoneme, occurring at the point of transition from Phoenician to Greek:

> "The adapter [from Phoenician to Greek] didn't seem to be certain of the orientation of the letters, because several were rotated or inverted. And for a collection of four related Phoenician sounds and letters – roughly equivalent to *z, s, ts,* and *sh* – the adapter exchanged sound, name, letter shape, and order. Here's what should have happened, if the adapter had made the most logical choices, compared to what actually happened:

Phoenician	Should have become	But actually became
Zei/z	San/s	Zeta/dz or sd or zd
Semek/s	Sigma/s	Xei/sh, later ks (x)
Sin/sh	Xei/sh	Sigma/s

Why these changes occurred has been the subject of highly complex research and arguments, incomprehensible to those unfamiliar with Arcado-Cypriot Labiovelar Palatalization and the like. But some details concern us here. Why, for instance, did *sh*, a sound that Phoenicians had but Greeks didn't, become *ks*? The *ks* combination could have been spelled perfectly well k+s [rather than *x*]. Why a separate letter? One possible answer is that Cypriot had originally had a *ks* as part of its syllabary.... [This] evidence [is] as good as any for placing the initial adapter [of Phoenician into Greek] ... on Cyprus." [4]

X is the twenty-fourth letter of the modern and the twenty-first letter of the ancient Roman alphabet, corresponding in form and position to the Greek X (*chi*). Circa 1000 BC, the Phoenicians and other Semites of Syria and Palestine began using X in the form of 丰, pronounced *samekh,* meaning fish, and used for their consonant "s." After 900 BC, the Greeks borrowed the sign and altered it slightly. The early Greek forms 王, 三, +, and X represented the aspirated voiceless velar (*kh*) in the Ionian alphabet, and (*ks*) in the Chalcidian alphabet. (In the former, [ks] was denoted by 三, in the latter, [kh] was denoted by 丫). /x/ in the International Phonetic Alphabet is pronounced *ch* as in German *buch* and *Reich* or Scottish *loch*.

There are three phonetic values of x in the English language. Words having initial x are pronounced /z/ in English and are nearly all of Greek origin. A few, as xebec and Xerez, have x representing early Spanish x (now *j*). The most common pronunciation is *ks* as in axis, buxom, oxen, tax. X was adopted by the Latins with the value *ks* from the Greek alphabet introduced into Italy. The pronunciation of x after a vowel or h varies somewhat depending on where it bears the stress (compare exile *ks* and exact or Alexander *gz*). Other irregularities in pronunciation are found in such words as luxury, anxious *ksh,* and luxurious *gzh.*

In Old English, x was used medially and finally as a variant spelling of *cs* (*sc*), e.g. fixian=fiscian (to fish). Initial x stands for *sh* (or *s*) in early forms of some words, as xerif (variant of sheriff after early Spanish *xerife*) and Xinto (Shinto). [5]

The early symbol for x, 丰, is reminiscent of the bones/spine of a fish. What possible mimetic similarity could there be between the phonetic and the symbol and the idea of fish? Before the establishment of alphabets, there were other arbitrary tools used to communicate with: sticks, knotted strings, bones, and shells were used as mnemonic signs (as opposed to pictographic) and therefore the bones of a fish might easily have been used for the very purpose of signaling an idea, an image, or even a sound. What could possibly be the repercussions of such a rebus-like linkage between thing, symbol, and letter. Cross bones in the form of an x still signify danger and death.

translator's preface

The "translation model of repression" (Laplanche) can be understood as a way to unravel the process of seduction resulting from a child's first contact with the adult world (the other). In "primal seduction" the adult interpellates the child with all types of enigmatic signifiers that the child must interpret (verbal, pictorial, gestural, and behavioural signifiers, not signs, for the meaning is as yet unknown). The process of translation on the child's part is doomed to "failure" for it is forced to resort to infantile (pre-linguistic) constructions of fantasy and trauma. Not only does the child not have the language and experience needed to translate these messages into something approaching their "original" intention, the messages coming from the other/adult are also compromised to begin with. The other is a fully constituted subject with its own conflicts and desires stemming from their unconscious. For the child, these messages coming from without are loaded with unconscious sexual meaning. The passivity and openness of the child to these new, unprecedented incoming messages is such that the "enigmatic signifiers," misconstrued and somatized within the "primitive body" of the child, take on a seductive and/or traumatic twist within the developing unconscious. As one grows out of this vulnerable position, these "enigmatic signifiers," stemming from one's first relations with an other, must be continuously retranslated into new situations. Desire and fear (guided by the hermeneutical process of condensation and displacement of images, words, and objects connecting the conscious to the unconscious in the production of meaning) must be retranslated through a reinterpretation of the "primal seduction" of the other. This "analysis" requires a process of psychic unbinding, the decomposition of subjective (egoic) and ideological formations so as to bring new relationships into play – new, non-repressive, non-exclusionary relationships. The internalized other as "enigmatic signifier" can be transferred outside to cultural sites, into performative, creative acts, that address and interpellate the other on other terms. This opening up and working through of what constitutes the "enigmatic signifier" translates the original seductive contact into new, intersubjective relations within the social sphere. The segmentation of speech/writing, the breakdown of the norms of syntax and structure, are but one way of translating internal/subjective and external/cultural signifiers so as to provide new ways of understanding the other and proffer new messages for the other in turn.

author's note

You find a letter, unopened, at the bottom of one of the many piles that comprise your desk. Something official. The envelope is opened. You begin to read it nonchalantly. But then, from far off, memory speaks. You break out in a sweat.

It's already too late. You're fucked. You've put it off for so long now it's not funny. You shouldn't have let it out of your sight. They'll be after you. And then it'll be all over. The possibilities ... the missed opportunities ... all that.... Christ, what an idiot you've been. It may be too late! The pen hovers, suspended above the yellowing paper. You, uncertain, read the small print ... or are you just pretending to? Thinking about how tedious the wording is. Must hurry ... oh fuck it. I may get caught, but then maybe I won't ... or is it just the finishing touches you are looking at, or the overall gestalt of the thing before you? But will they acknowledge it? Is it worth bothering to finalize with the usual flourish? Or would it be better off a crumpled projectile headed for the waste bin? Perhaps you are merely signing a cheque, a passport, a piece of ID. Or maybe you are before a legal contract of some sort. You are deciding whether to agree with the laws, the stipulations, the exceptions and irregularities, the mandate, the clause, the philosophy, the adopted cause.... It is more likely that you are doing something illegal, slush funds, illegal investment, embezzlement, authorizing a trade agreement that will land you millions. Maybe you began to read over the contract carefully and then proceeded to skim the rest in embarrassment (feeling that it was taking too long, the language tedious, the print too fine, your brain lazy). You are on the verge of buying something, supporting something, selling something, renting something, signing something over to somebody, signing your life over to somebody. Or maybe the decision was already made a long time in advance. You are deliberating over how to sign. Neatly and calmly, as if in no hurry. Quickly, forcefully, and with determination and finality. How will you represent yourself within this legal act? This will belong to you. You will belong to them. It will own you. Or maybe it will belong to you no more. A mere act of authoring. A gain. A loss. As a rule, your signature should be consistent with all the rest of your signatures. It will no doubt be scrutinized at some future moment for authentification. A flourish should end your personal squiggle. Or a line of daggers marching across the line. Illegibility – the sign of a busy important life or a fiery personality. A shaky start – a half-wit. Make sure it fits. You make yourself. Even in a signature. Let it be you. Become you. It's a starting point. Once it's done, it should be quickly forgotten. There's nothing to be done now. Might as well open a vein if you have any regrets. Or go into a life of crime and erase your former identity completely. The die is cast. On the other hand, if you have refused to sign your name, or just hastily threw away that piece of paper, you are probably further ahead than the rest of us. (Or if you can't read or write, don't worry about it and just sign with an x.) We are all best represented thus, each individual stream of ink following the same dream. Just so long as you've got something to contribute to the game. Follow the rules. Keep in check. Sign up before it's too late. Reap your rewards. You deserve it. You're an individual with a great name. And you are indispensable to the cause, the order of things.

But wait. No. That will no longer do. Your hand and our eye are not good enough. Let's take a photograph, certify everything before a notary public; let's have a letter addressed to you from an important firm; let's have your credit history, your fingerprints, your iris patterns, some DNA samples, your PIN and SIN numbers, your password. Now let's enter them all into your personal file, traceable by all insurance agencies and credit bureaus. And, lest we forget – could you please sign your name here on this digital document. From now on, this is the legal template of all future signatures. You are now all caught up with the times. You can throw that slip of paper away. You are now part of electronic history. [6]

symbols and abbreviations [7]

24th letter of the alphabet.

The letter or its sound.

The letter considered with regard to its shape. Hence identified with a cross. *X's and O's:* the game of noughts and crosses.

Any unknown or unnamed factor, thing, or person.

The person in question: used especially by an illiterate person in place of a signature.

Something (as a statement, answer, or result) that is wrong; a mistake or error.

Opposition, confrontation, annulment, obstruction, mistake, cancellation, the unknown, unfamiliar, undecided, unsettled, nonsensical.

In mathematics: a. An unknown number; b. An algebraic variable; c. The multiplication symbol.

The Roman numeral ten.

Power of magnification.

To delete, cancel, or obliterate with a series of x's.

Used to indicate a mechanical defect in type.

Placed on a map or diagram to mark the location or position of a point.

Seen in old photographs to indicate a known person, now dead or unrecognizable from aging.

A playing card of low rank.

Choice (on a ballot paper).

Indicating a motion picture rating of such nature that no one under a certain age (usually 16–18) is to be admitted (rated X).

A symbol for Christ or Christian.

The symbol for a kiss.

His/her mark.

In divorce cases, x refers to the consenting but undisclosed Miss, Ms, Mrs, or Mr involved in the adulterous relationship/affair.

Hoarfrost (meteorol).

Northumberland (B.V.R.).

Used in street names to designate cross (e.g., King's X).

Used as a secret code word (letter) for when one is talking about marijuana or amphetamines, etc.

The name of a hold used, for instance, by a police officer on a criminal, whereby the latter is held by their shirt collar while their arm is twisted back such that if the criminal tries to break free it is easy for the officer to break the criminal's arm. Called an x because of the cross position of the arm behind the back.

The number 1,000 in ancient Greece.

Symbol for Chronos, the god of time, and the planet Saturn in Greek and Roman mythology.

Bold **X** stands for the cross of St. Andrew.

Symbol for talc in 17th-century alchemy.

In musical notation, X means double sharp.

English hobo sign meaning "Don't knock here."

One of the oldest signs. Like +, it is found scratched on the walls of prehistoric caves in Europe and Central America. Ideographically it is believed that x is more closely related to two arrows meeting each other, ↑, than to +.

In early Chinese ideography x stood for the number 5. One was to count not only the directionality of each arm, but the centre as well.

As an Egyptian hieroglyph it meant divide, count, and break into parts. This is interesting when one considers that it was used as a multiplication sign from the 17th century on.

A narrow X is a rune by the name of *gif* or *geba* used in old Nordic rune alphabets. It means gift, especially from a chief or warrior.

It can also be used as a symbol in the crossbreeding of different species or races, in chess (takes), ground-to-air emergency codes (cannot continue), and road obstruction (military).

X a ten-dollar note; XX a twenty dollar note (*U.S. colloq.*)

x ex.; extra

X experiment; explosive; extension

x.a. ex all

XACT X (unnamed computer) automatic code translation

xbt exhibit

x.c. ex capitalization

x.c.l. excess current liabilities

xcpt except

x.cut cross cut

x.cy cross country

x.d., x/d., x.div. ex dividend, not including right to dividend

x'd executed

x.dr. ex drawings

xdr crusader

Xe symbol for the element xenon

X.E. experimental engine

X-er someone who is from the X generation

Xer. Xerox reproduction

x.f. extra fine

xfa. cross-fired acceleration

xfer transfer

Xgam. experimental guided air missile

XH Honduras (*ICAM*); experimental helicopter

XHMO extended huckel molecular orbit

xhst exhaust

x.hvy extra heavy

XI Belfast (*vehicle registration*)

x.i. ex (without) interest

XL extra large

xlnt, x/nt excellent

X.M. experimental missile

XML extensible markup language; a meta-data system language, similar to HTML but far more sophisticated

Xn Christian; **Xnty** Christianity

XO a cognac of superior quality

X-O test a psychological test for the investigation of emotional attitudes in which the subject is required to cross out certain words and, repeating the test, circle one word in each line

XP a monogram used to represent Christ or Christianity, composed of *chi* and *rho*, the first two letters of the Greek word for Christ

xpl. explosive

xplt exploit

xpn expansion

x.q. cross question

Xr *Also* **Xber.** December *(Obs.)*

x. roads cross roads

x.ref. cross reference

x.rts without rights

xs expenses

XTC slang for the drug Ecstasy

xtran. experimental language (computer)

XUV extreme ultra violet

XX, XXX in designating brands of ale, stout or porter, *XX* denotes a medium quality, *XXX* the strongest quality

XXX characterizes explicit sexual representation in film, video, and other interactive media

XXX symbol for Amsterdam

xyz the introduction of x, y, z as symbols or unknown quantities is due to Déscartes who, in order to provide symbols of unknowns corresponding to the symbols a, b, c of knowns, took the last letter of the alphabet, z, for the first unknown and proceeded backwards to y and x for the second and third unknowns respectively. There is no evidence in support of the hypothesis that x is derived ultimately from the mediaeval transliteration *xei* or *shei* "thing," used by the Arabs to denote the unknown quantity or from the compendium for L. *res* "thing" or *radix* "root" (resembling a loosely-written x), used by Mediaeval mathematicians.

xyz examine your zipper

XYZ some thing or person unknown or undetermined

Petrified unrest; a life which knows no development.

quotations

There are no resemblances without signatures. The world of similarity can only be a world of signs. Paracelsus says: 'It is not God's
will that what he creates for man's benefit and what he has given
us should remain hidden…. And even though he has hidden certain things, he has allowed nothing to remain without exterior and
visible signs in the form of special marks – just as a man who
has buried a hoard of treasure marks the spot that he may find it
again.' A knowledge of similitudes is founded upon the unearthing
and decipherment of these signatures…. The system of signatures
reverses the relation of the visible to the invisible. Resemblance
was the invisible form of that which, from the depths of the world,
made things visible…. This is why the face of the world is covered
with blazons, with characters, with ciphers and obscure words –
with 'hieroglyphics,' as Turner called them. And the space inhabited
by immediate resemblances becomes like a vast open book. [8]

The first diagonal marks the progress of a language from the point
of view of its specification; the second [diagonal marks] the endless interleaving of language and representation – the duplicating
process which is the reason why the verbal sign is always representing a representation. On this latter line, the word functions
as a substitute (with its power to represent); on the former, as an
element (with its power to make combinations and break them

down). At this point where these two diagonals intersect, at the centre of the quadrilateral, where the duplicating process of representation is revealed as analysis, where the substitute has the power of distribution, and where in consequence, there resides the possibility and the principle of a general taxonomy of representation, there is the name. To name is at the same time to give the verbal representation of a representation, and to place it in a general table. The entire Classical theory of language is organized around this central and privileged entity. [9]

– Michel Foucault, *Les mots et les choses*

X in our alphabet being a needless letter has an added invincibility to the attacks of the spelling reformers, and like them, will doubtless last as long as the language. X is the sacred symbol of ten dollars, and in such words as Xmas, Xn, etc., stands for Christ, not, as is popularly supposed, because it represents a cross, but because the corresponding letter in the Greek alphabet is the initial of His name – *Xpiotos*. If it represented a cross it would stand for St. Andrew, who 'testified' upon one of the shapes. In the algebra of psychology x stands for Woman's mind. Words beginning with X are Grecian and will not be defined in this standard English dictionary. [10]

– Ambrose Bierce, *Devil's Dictionary*

Psychoanalysis' space, the space of the unconscious … disdains this fundamental notion of the coordinates of the real. In defiance of all probability it allows two, or three, or five things to be in the same place at the same time. And these things are themselves utterly heteroclite, not variations on one another but things in total opposition. This 'space' is therefore quite literally unimaginable: a congealed block of contradictions. Not a function of the visible, it can only be intuited through the projection of various 'figures' that surface from the depths of this 'space': the slip of the tongue, the daydream, the fantasy. To this medium, lying below the level of the visible, he gives the name matrix, and he begins to follow its activity, which he recognizes as the production not of the gestalt but of bad form, the activity through which form is in fact transgressed.... Structuralism, grounding its own truth in the laws of opposition between binary pairs, is fond of the principle of commutability. In the abstract, logical space of the table in which S is contrasted with $\bar{S}$, it makes no difference if $\bar{S}$ were to precede its opposite. The commutability is an equally neutral affair for the linguist, who says that a transformation into the passive is correct if it changes nothing in the meaning; thus, 'X beats a child' is the same as 'a child is being beaten by X'. But unlike the linguist, the analyst has seen desire sneaking through the space of this diagram, trying to escape attention by ... following the rules. 'At the very interior of this legitimate transformation wholly contained within the system of oppositions,' Lyotard marvels, 'the thrust of an anal-sadistic regression toward masochistic pleasure is nonetheless represented.' The analyst, caring nothing for the logic of commutability's 'no change,' has spotted the way desire has put the innocence of syntax to work so that the 'neutral' fact of the passive voice might carry the psychic meaning implied by a retreat from action. The activity of 'X beats the child' is genital, the expression of Oedipal desire, as the girl identifies with her father. But as the repression of this desire and its release of guilt transports the watching patient into the place of the (other) child, passive, she now assumes the role of victim. Yet the masochism of this position has its own reward, as a spanking that is also understood as a caress hastens a regressive debasement in the libidinal nature of the drive. [11] [For more on Krauss' reflections on the relationship between formalist theories in art and the construction of desire in psychoanalytic theory see Appendix D.]

– Rosalind Krauss, *The Optical Unconscious*

In a country that's in a hurry to make the future, the names attached to the products are an enduring reassurance. Johnson & Johnson and Quaker State and RCA Victor and Burlington Mills and Bristol-Myers and General Motors. These are the venerated emblems of the burgeoning economy, easier to identify than the names of battlefields or dead presidents. [12]

– Don Delillo, *Underworld*

With this wave of brand mania has come a new breed of business-man, one who will proudly inform you that Brand X is not a product but a way of life, an attitude, a set of values, a look, an idea. And it sounds really great – way better than that Brand X is a screwdriver, or a hamburger chain, or a pair of jeans, or even a very successful line of running shoes. Nike, Phil Knight announced in the late eighties, is 'a sports company'; its mission is not to sell shoes but to 'enhance people's lives through sports and fitness' and to keep 'the magic of sports alive.' Company president-cum-speaker-shaman Tom Clark explains that 'the inspiration of sports allows us to rebirth ourselves constantly.' [13]

– Naomi Klein, *No Logo*

Graffiti points towards a secret about identity under capital – the sacrifice of human qualities for renown and tradeability. [14]

– Julian Stallabrass, *Gargantua*

proper names [15]

(additional names found in sections: xeno- and image, music, text)

X, Malcolm Born Malcolm Little on May 19, 1925 in Omaha, Nebraska. His parents were both members of Marcus Garvey's Universal Negro Improvement Association (UNIA). Family driven from Omaha by the Ku Klux Klan. After his father's death and mother's mental breakdown, he was sent to several foster homes. In Boston, Malcolm was imprisoned for burglary. In prison, he was introduced to the Nation of Islam. He was drawn to the Black nationalist practices, in particular its gift for rehabilitating black male prisoners, its interest in empowering the poor, its emphasis on black pride, history, culture. He was an intransigent opponent of the U.S. government and its imperialist policies. He fought the racist oppression of Blacks and the profit-driven exploitation of Africa, Asia, and Latin America. He expressed this revolutionary outlook in the opening years of the 1960s while a major spokesperson for the Nation of Islam. He preached the militant Islamic doctrine of Elijah Muhammed, calling for racial segregation and affirming the superiority of Blacks over whites in view of abolishing white supremacy and of refashioning broken strands between Afro-American and African culture. Following his March 1964 break with the Nation, Malcolm's views continued to evolve – first in an anti-capitalist, and then in a pro-socialist direction. He also revised his opinions about white men being the devil. During the last years of his life, he organized the Muslim Mosque and the Organization of Afro-American

.S.
.A.
.S. M .S.
X   ÿ
.
X͞po FERENS·//

Unity (OAAU). He spent much of the last year of his life in Africa and the Middle East observing, speaking, and meeting with political leaders there. He was gunned down by Nation of Islam loyalists as he was preparing to speak at an OAAU meeting on February 21, 1965.

Xai-Xai A port town in southern Mozambique. It is a market centre for cashew nuts, rice, corn, cassava, and sorghum. Cattle are also raised.

Xaintrie A physical region in France, in the Massif Central, a plateau region in the south.

Xalvaquiej A hamlet about 150 kilometres northwest of Guatemala City.

Xankandi Formerly Stepanakert, a city in southwestern Azerbaijan. Situated at the foot of the eastern slopes of the Karabakj Range, the city was founded after the October Revolution in 1917 on the site of the village of Khankendy and was renamed Stepanakert in 1923 for Stepan Shaumyan, a Baku Communist Leader. After Azerbaijan gained independence, the name was changed to Xankandi.

Xanthi A city and department in the Thrace region of eastern Greece. The city is the seat of a metropolitan bishop of the Greek Orthodox church. Originally, it grew up beneath the Byzantine fortress of Xanthea and later became a summer colony of the Turks. After the Balkan Wars (1912-13) the city passed to Bulgaria and then Greece after World War I.

Xanthippe 1. The wife of Socrates; proverbial as a shrewish and scolding woman. 2. The daughter of Dorus (son of Apollo and Phthia). She married Pleuron.

Xanthippus 1. The father of Pericles. 2. Spartan army general in the first Punic war.

Xantho One of the Oceanids, ocean nymphs held to be the daughters of Oceanus and Tethys.

Xanthos A Lydian historian from Ancient Greek times.

Xanthus 1. Xanthus and Balius were the immortal horses of Achilles, the Greek hero of the Trojan War. They were the offspring of Zephyrus, the west wind, and a harpy named Podarge (meaning "fleet-foot"). 2. Modern day Kinik. An ancient city on the Xanthus river about eight miles above its mouth in what is now western Turkey. In the 6th century BC it was the principal city of Lycia. About 540 BC it was besieged by Harpagus, general of the Persian king Cyrus. The Lycians, forced within their walls, collected their wives and children and burned them, together with their slaves and treasure; then, attacking the Persians, they all perished. The city was rebuilt and flourished until 42 BC when it was besieged by the Romans under the command of Brutus. The most remarkable ruins of the city are huge, rock-cut pillar tombs; upon one of these is the longest and most important of inscriptions in the Lycian language.

Xavier, Saint Francis Born April 7, 1506, at Xavier Castle, near Sanguesa, Navarre, Spain. The most famous Roman Catholic missionary of all modern times, he was instrumental in the establishment of Christianity in India, the Malay Archipelago, and Japan. In Paris in 1534 he pronounced vows as one of the first seven members of the Society of Jesus, or Jesuits, under the leadership of Ignatius of Loyola. Died in 1552. Canonized in 1622.

Xauen Also Chechaouene, town in Morocco.

Xena The heroic protagonist of the TV show *Xena: Warrior Princess*. Reminiscent of such TV female action hero archetypes of the '70s as Wonder Woman and the Bionic Woman, but "updated" by being set in a mythical past.

Xenia A city in southwestern Ohio, U.S., founded in 1803 by Joseph C. Vance who gave it a Greek name meaning "hospitality."

Xenocrates Greek philosopher, pupil of Plato, and successor of Speusippus as the head of the Greek Academy, which Plato founded in 387 BC. In the company of Aristotle he left Athens after Plato's death in 348-347 BC, returning in 339 BC on his election as head of the Academy where he remained until his death. His writings are lost except for fragments, but his doctrines appear to resemble Plato's. Among them is the "derivation" of all reality from the interaction of two opposing principles, "the One" and "the indeterminate dyad." It is the dyad that is responsible for multiplicity, or diversity, evil, and motion. The One is responsible for unity, good, and rest. He divided all of reality into three realms: the sensibles, the intelligibles (Plato's Ideas), and the bodies of the heavens which mediate between the sensibles and the intelligibles. Another threefold division separates gods, men, and demons. His demonology was highly influential on early Christian writers who identified pagan deities with evil demons. The classical distinction differentiating mind, body, and soul has been attributed by some to Xenocrates, by others to the Stoic philosopher Poseidonius. He divides philosophy into three categories: logic, physics, and ethics. The origin of philosophy he says lies in man's desire to resolve his anxieties. Happiness is defined as the acquisition of the perfection that is peculiar to "man."

Xenodice In Greek mythology, one of Minos and Pasiphae's daughters. Ariadne's sister.

Xenolophus Name of a district in Byzantium (now Istanbul).

Xenophanes c.560-478 BC. Greek poet and rhapsodist, religious thinker, and reputed precursor of the Eleatic school of philosophy, which stressed unity rather than diversity and viewed the separate existences of material things as apparent rather than real. His philosophy begins from the principle of the unity of all things. His teaching can be summed up by the formula: "The all is one and the one is God."

Xenophon. Greek general and historian, 431-350 BC. Author of *Anabasis*, a book that became a bible for 19th- and early 20th-century imperialism. *Anabasis* describes how European Greeks fought against and conquered large numbers of assorted Asiatics. The Latin equivalent to Xenophon's text is Caesar's *Gallic Wars*.

Xerox A trademark for a photocopying process or machine using xerography.

Xerox Corporation A major U.S. corporation and first manufacturer of xerographic, plain-paper copiers. Headquartered in Stamford, Connecticut, the company was founded in 1906 as Haloid Company, changed its name to Haloid Xerox in 1958, and to Xerox Corporation in 1961. In 1960, Xerox first marketed the 914 Xerographic copier. The product was so successful that the company has had to wage an ongoing campaign to prevent the trademark Xerox from becoming a generic term.

Xerox PARC Xerox Palo Alto Research Center. Founded in California in 1970, it helped develop GUIs, object-oriented programming languages, Ethernet LANs, laser printers, and specific technologies for Xerox copiers and printers. Xerox PARC's motto: "The easiest way to predict the future is to invent it."

Xerxes I Also Xerxes the Great, King of Persia (486-465 BC). Etymologically, from Old Persian *Khshaayarshan*, meaning "ruling over men." He was son and successor of Darius I and was best known for his massive invasion of Greece from across the Hellespont in 480 BC. His ultimate defeat spelled the beginning of the decline of the Achaemenid Empire.

XFL The Extreme Football League was started by Vince McMahon, mastermind behind the World Wrestling Federation; lasted only about three months; extinct as of May 2001.

Xhemal Pasha Past ruler of lands which stretched from Kruje to the border of the other great warrior tribe of the north, the Catholic Mirdite

(Albania). Father to Zogu, who became king of the Albanians in 1928.

Xhyuu Name of a Xhaadydla (Haida) poet whose oral narratives were transcribed by John Reed Swanton around 1900.

Xi Jiang The longest river of southern China.

Xi Kang Chinese Taoist philosopher, alchemist, and poet (223-262 AD). He was one of the most important members of the free-spirited, heavy drinking Seven Sages of the Bamboo Grove, a coterie of poets and philosophers who scandalized Chinese society by their iconoclastic thoughts and actions.

Xi Xia A kingdom of the Tibetan-speaking Tangut tribes, established in the 11th century, and which flourished through the early 13th century. It was located in what are now the northwestern Chinese provinces of Kansu and Shensi. The Xi Xia dynasty was conquered by the Mongol troops of Genghis Khan in 1227.

Xia (Hsi) dynasty An early Chinese dynasty (22nd-19/18th century BC; traditional dates c. 2205-c. 1766 BC) described in legends, but it is uncertain as to its historicity. The founder was named Yu, who engineered the draining of the waters of a great flood (becoming deified as lord of the harvest). Yu made rule hereditary in his family, founding the first imperial dynasty in China. There is archeological evidence that the Xia dynasty fell after the eruption of the volcano Thera, thus facilitating the overthrow of the Xia by the Shang dynasty.

Xia Gui One of China's greatest masters of landscape painting, 1195-1224. Cofounder with Ma Yuan of the Ma-Hsia school. The album leaf and the hand scroll with a continuous panorama were his predominant forms.

Xiang Jiang A river in Hunan province, China. Running 500 miles in length, it is one of the principal tributaries of the Yangtze River.

Xiang Yu 232-202 BC. Chinese general and leader of the rebel forces that overthrew the Ch'in dynasty (221-206 BC). He was the principal contestant for control of China with Liu Pang, the founder of the Han dynasty (206 BC-220 AD). Xiang Yu's defeat signaled the end of the old aristocratic order in China.

Xiangkhoang A town in north-central Laos.

Xiangtan A city in eastern Hunan province in China.

Xianyang A city in Shensi province, China.

Xiaowen Di Emperor of the Northern Wei dynasty (386-534), which dominated much of northern China during part of the chaotic 360-year period between the end of the Han dynasty and the founding of Sui rule. Xiaowen Di sinicized his tribal kinsmen, making the Northern Wei into a Chinese-style dynasty. He also instituted a land-reform program that has persisted in its basic form into modern times.

Xie He Chinese figure painter best remembered as the critic who invented or collated the "Six Principles" of Chinese painting.

Xin Dynasty A short-lived dynasty in China, 9-25 AD, formed by Wang Mang.

Xin Qiji Chinese poet and master soldier, 1140-1207, whose *tz'u* (poems written to existing musical patterns) are considered by many critics to be the best of the Southern Sung dynasty.

Xingu A river of Brazil, rising in central Mato Grosso and flowing 1,230 miles generally north to the Amazon.

Xiong Foxi Chinese playwright, 1900-1965, who helped to create popular drama intended to entertain and educate the peasantry.

Xiong Shili One of the outstanding figures of 20th-century Chinese philosophy. His ontological system is an original synthesis of Buddhist, Confucian, and Western motifs.

Xiphilinus, Johannes Epitomator of Dio Cassius. Lived at Constantinople during the latter half of the 11th century. He was a monk and the nephew of the patriarch of Constantinople of the same name.

Xirgu, Margarita Catalan actress and producer, 1888-1969. One of her greatest contributions was her advancement of the plays of Federico Garcia Lorca.

Xisouthros Greek hero of the flood and possessor of the secret of immortality. Also known as Utnapishtim (Mesopotamia) and Ziusudra (Sumeria).

Xouthos The father of Ion, legendary eponym after whom one of the primary tribes of Greece were named. It is believed to be phonetically derived from the Semitic Seth. This name may well come from confusion with the Canaanite Sid – the god of sea and hunting – and therefore related to Poseidon, who not so coincidentally was the patron god of the Ionians.

Xoxe, Koci Albanian leader who, along with Enver Hoxha, agreed to have their country absorbed as a seventh republic into Yugoslavia.

Xu Xing Contemporary Chinese writer, best known for his book *Variations without a theme and other stories.*

Xuthus In Greek mythology, a son of Hellen, and the ancestor of the Ionian Greeks.

XY Company Canadian trading company, founded in 1802. Also known as the New North West Company or Sir Alexander Mackenzie and Company.

Xylopolis Ancient city in Macedonia.

Xyniae Ancient city in Thessaly.

Xyron A patented adhesive/lamination system.

Xystus Name of popes; also Sixtus I, II, and III.

THE PROPER

"Thus the subject, too, if it can appear to be the slave of language, is all the more so the slave of a discourse in the universal movement in which its place is already inscribed at birth, if only by virtue of its proper name." [16]

"Writing can never be thought under the category of the subject; however it is modified, however it is endowed with consciousness or unconsciousness, it will refer, by the entire thread of its history, to the substantiality of a presence unperturbed by accidents, or to the identity of the selfsame [le propre] in the presence of self-relationship. And the thread of that history clearly does not run within the borders of metaphysics. To determine an X as a subject is never an operation of a pure convention, it is never an indifferent gesture in relation to writing. Spacing as writing is the becoming-absent and the becoming-unconscious of the subject. By the movement of its drift/derivation [dérive] the emancipation of the sign constitutes in return the desire of presence.... As the subject's relationship with its own death, this becoming is the constitution of subjectivity. On all levels of life's organization, that is to say, of the economy of death. All graphemes are of a testamentary essence. And the original absence of the subject of writing is also the absence of the thing or the referent." [17]

The proper, as in property, personal, particular, owning, belonging, appropriateness, thoroughness, "worthy of the name," fit, meeting a standard of competence, correctness, and cleanliness [French: *propre*].

According to Walter Benjamin, naming is to human knowledge what the word is to divine creation (*In the beginning was the word….*). He says that naming is limited and analytical in nature, based on convention rather than anything innately proper to the character of beings/things. But there is one exception: "… the point where human language participates most intimately in the divine infinity of the pure word, the point at which it cannot become finite word and language, are the human name. The theory of proper names is that theory of the frontier between finite and infinite language."

When a child is born, one cannot know this being's nature, not before it has begun to learn to communicate with an as yet unknown world. Considering language pre-exists the infant, and considering how language's structure and its ideological habits mould thought throughout one's development into a social identity, the proper name functions as *the* initiatory and symbolic act that grounds the individual within tradition, religion, community, nation, class, gendered identity. It does not impart any innate meaning to the child, except perhaps for some symbolic meaning that the parent wishes to project. The initiation fills in for a nameless and unknowable fate. A clean slate is marked first and foremost by the proper. The proper name becomes a stamp of belonging: one has one's surname but also one's given name. There is individualism, the self-same, and then there is the sense of taking one's place on the branch of a larger tree, a cultivated one (through the family name, and other future titles attached to the name), a "tree of knowledge" as such. In this respect, naming is a performative act. It is an act of symbolic investiture. A private or official act of interpellation into a given social identity. From the moment someone or something is named or given a title, she/he/it is inscribed within a pre-existing order, hierarchy, habitus.

In a secular context, first names like "John" and "Mary" float inter-changeably between individuals marked by the same appellation. The proper name is fungible. In certain rare cases a first name takes on perennial characteristics: Jesus, Elvis, etc.; last names do this with even more frequency: Freud, Marx, etc. In the religious context and in certain non-Western and/or "pre-colonized" societies, naming and meaning relate more to a collective cultural system rather than to the assertion of individuality. In the case of certain "tribal" cultures, proper names cannot be uttered, only replacement names or nicknames (cf. Claude Levi-Strauss' *La vie familiale et sociale des Indiens Nambik-wara*). Or a dead person's name must be banished from the spoken vocabulary. This recalls the taboo within Judaism which forbids one to speak the name of God, Yahweh, replacing it in speech with Adonai. Or you have a secular name and a religious name, having different functions. Within naming is a complicated structuring of moral law and transgression. Names contain within them a particular "magic." The name and the individual grow together, forming a third meaning.

That is unless the individual later decides to reject the given/aquired name and take on a new one. This tends to be a transgressive act in terms of defying the institutions of nation and family. A Chinese daughter may be named Zhang Xiaomei. She moves to Vancouver and her parents change her name to Christina Zhang. This name change marks the symbolic appropriation of a new nationality. Then, when she is older, in a gesture of frustration, confusion, and anti-patriarchal sentiment she officially changes her name to an androgynous Max Henze, a combination of Latin and Germanic roots. There is a fracturing of meaning and loss of history, a marking of difference and a loss of difference in this gesture. Former symbolic acts of investiture are held up as suspect. Caught between cultures one decides to belong to a new culture of narcissism, or of a new "tribalism." Marcel Duchamp sometimes went by Rrose Selavy, performing a gender transformation based on a play on words. In the case of Malcolm X, there is a purposeful rejection of a surname based on prior colonial violence and cultural dispossession. In Honduras, some peasant parents give absurd and obscene first names to their children: Motor, Ignition, Bujia (Spark Plug), Defecacion Flores (Defecation Flowers), Llanta de Milagro (Miracle Tire), even Bill Clinton and Ronald Reagan. This also seems to have something to do with being culturally dispossessed and could be seen as a poignant symptom of what happens to identity under the overriding logic of capital.

The proper name distances the subject from the other, reinforcing the gap between you and me. The individual takes on the family surname, the name of the parent (usually the name of the father), plus another that distinguishes oneself further, the first name (self-sameness). The shared family name signals prohibition (the laws of kinship/incest taboo), marking the difference between nature and culture. Our pets, some laboratory animals, a few famous anthropological bipeds, are also given proper names. So are mountains, rivers, cities, as they are charted or constructed. Even hurricanes (there is a wind named Xlokk). The proper name is also an appropriation of nature. In that act of possession something dies and becomes other. The proper name that signals nature is therefore not about the self-same but about what is "ours" or "theirs."

Language, as writing, is grounded in violence, on rupture (*via rupta*). The history of language, of writing, in some ways could be seen as the history of roads, mapping, and conquest, the violent spacing of nature through agriculture, then city planning, the violent spacing of the forest that destroys a former way of life. As Derrida states: "… it is difficult to imagine that access to the possibility of a road-map is not at the same time access to writing." [18] The ploughing of the field corresponds to the invention of language. Perhaps that is why the first letter of our alphabet is the ox head, also resembling an upside down plough. A cultivation of knowledge and a search for efficiency. Being able to call it your own.

music, image, text [19]

X Punk band formed in Los Angeles in 1977: Exene Cervenka (vocals), Billy Zoom (guitar), John Doe (bass), Mick Basher (drums; replaced by D.J. Bonebrake). Their musical style was a blend of punk, rock-a-billy and blues. Major labels were unreceptive to the group until independent Slash signed them in 1979. Albums: *Los Angeles* (Slash 1980), *Wild Gift* (Slash 1981), *The Decline ... of Western Civilization* soundtrack (Slash 1981), *Under the Big Black Sun* (Elektra 1982), *More Fun In The World* (Elektra 1983), *Ain't Love Grand* (Elektra 1985), *See How We Are* (Elektra 1987), *Live at the Whisky A Go-Go on the Fabulous Sunset Strip* (Elektra 1988), *Major League* soundtrack (Curb 1989), *Hey Zeus!* (Big Life/Mercury 1993), *Unclogged* (Infidelity 1995). As well as X, Cervenka and Doe joined the country-rock band the Knitters. Dave Alvin replaced Zoom after *Ain't Love Grand*, but left in 1987. Ex-Lone Justice guitarist Tony Gilkyson also joined. X disbanded after *Live at the Whisky A Go-Go* but reunited for *Hey Zeus* in 1993. In 1998 they were on the road again after the release of a set of live recordings.

Generation X A British punk group formed in 1976 in London: Billy Idol (vocals, ex-Chelsea), Tony James (bass/vocals; ex-Chelsea), Bob Andrews (guitar/vocals), and John Towe (drums; replaced by Mark Laff in 1977). Signed to the Chrysalis label. Scraped the U.K. chart with *Your Generation* and *Ready Steady Go*. Following *Friday's Angels* (1979), Terry Chimes (ex-Clash) replaced Laff. Biggest commercial success was *King Rocker* (1979). Group lasted until 1981. Idol went solo,

John Towe joined the Adverts, Terry Chimes rejoined the Clash, and Tony James reinvented himself in Sigue Sigue Sputnik.

Xmal Deutschland An experimental/atmospheric band, formed in Hamburg, Germany in 1980: Anja Huwe (vocals), Manuela Rickers (guitar), Fiona Sangster (keyboards). Original members Rita Simon and Caro May replaced by Wolfgang Ellerbrock (bass) and Manuela Zwingmann (drums). Songs sung in German. Went to England in 1982 to support the Cocteau Twins. Joined 4AD Records soon after. Albums: *Fetisch* (4AD 1982), *Tocsin* (4AD 1984).

X-Ray Spex Band that began performing in the U.K. in 1977: punk icon Poly Styrene (vocals), Lora Logic (saxophone; later replaced by Glyn Johns), Jak Stafford (guitar), Paul Dean (bass), B.P. Hurding (drums). Part of their second gig was captured on the seminal *Live at the Roxy WC2*. It played high energy punk with thought-provoking lyrics. The band dismantled in 1979 and Poly Styrene joined the Krishna Consciousness Movement. The band reunited in 1996 for the release of a new album. Albums: *Germ Free Adolescents* (EMI 1978), *Conscious Consumer* (Receiver 1996).

XTC This British band that formed in 1972 in Wiltshire, England, was first known as Star Park (Rats Krap backwards), then Helium Kidz in 1973, and finally XTC in 1975-76: Andy Partridge (guitar/vocals), Colin Moulding (bass/vocals), Terry Chambers (drums), Dave Cartner (guitar), Barry Andrews (keyboards). The band emerged during the punk-new wave explosion and had a strong cult following on both sides of the Atlantic. It signed with Virgin in 1977. Albums: *3-D* (1977), *White Music* (1978), *Go 2* (1978), *Drums and Wires* (1979), *Black Sea* (1980), *English Settlement* (1982), *Mummer* (1983), *The Big Express* (1984), *Skylarking* (1986), *Oranges and Lemons* (1989), *Nonsuch* (1992). In 1982, Partridge, suffering from illness due to exhaustion and nervous breakdowns, announced that XTC would continue only as recording artists, avoiding the stage. [20]

Xenakis, Iannis Born a Greek in Romania in 1922, Xenakis was trained in architecture in Athens. Between 1947 and 1959, he worked with Le Corbusier, reportedly contributing to the spatial installation of Edgard Varese's *Poème electronique* at the 1958 Brussels World's Fair. While working in architecture, he studied music with Olivier Messiaen and Darius Milhaud. Using various kinds of mathematics, Xenakis advocated what Nicolas Slonimsky calls "the stochastic method" which is teleologically directed and deterministic, as distinct from a purely aleatory (i.e., John Cagean) handling of data. Xenakis also founded and directed the Centre d'Etudes Mathematiques et Automatiques Musicales in Paris (and for a while a comparable Centre for Mathematical and Automated Music in the U.S.), purportedly in competition with Pierre Boulez's IRCAM. All the theory notwithstanding, one can hear thickly atonal texture, which sound like bands of frequencies in the tradition of tone clusters, often distributed among many loudspeakers. For the French pavilion at Montreal's Expo '67, Xenakis also created, as an accompaniment to his audiotape, a spatially extended flickering light show. He died in 2001. [21]

X for Henry Flynt (also titled *Arabic Numeral (Any Integer) for Henry Flynt*) (1960). This musical score by Lamonte Young requires the performer to play an unspecified sound, or group of sounds, in a distinct and consistent rhythmic pattern for as long as the performer wishes. Young's first performance of this piece consisted of 600-odd beats on a frying pan. At a later date he played a discordant chord on the piano 1,698 times. This piece is very important historically because it was the precursor to minimalist composers' use of repetition in their music. [22]

Xhafa, Sislej A contemporary Albanian artist, born in Peja, Kosovo, whose work reflects the stereotypes of Albania as a land of mafia criminals, terrorists, and violence. He now works in Italy and New York, but his work always reflects on his status as suspicious foreigner. He acts as a clandestine in most of his works, using a mixture of poor materials and expensive ones, like mixing cheap jewelry and expensive furniture in an imitation of a gangster-like lifestyle. Some of his better known performances include dressing up as a commodities trader and improvising a stock exchange auction in front of a billboard announcing the arrival and departure of trains. This becomes a comment on the bureaucracy of everyday life, with its visas, customs officers, and the complex monetary exchanges and systems of trade between countries. In a public installation in Ghent, Xhafa transforms the lobby of a police station into a high class hotel, so that illegal immigrants can get one last chance at experiencing a mirage of wealth and success before being taken to prison or being deported back to their homeland. In *Again, Again* he had an entire orchestra play classical music outdoors while wearing balaclavas. His most recent piece (2001), entitled *Illegal Casino,* takes place in the Swiss Institute in New York. The installation has a gritty shady atmosphere, lit only by the coloured lights of slot machines. A possible interpretation: dirty money is recycled in Swiss banks. [23]

Xu Bing A contemporary Chinese artist, born in Beijing in 1955. Best known for his works "A case study of transference" (installation/video of two pigs rutting and interacting in a pigpen filled with Xu's books; one pig is covered in Xu's invented characters and the other in English letters) and "A book from the sky" (an installation of books and scrolls printed with Xu's invented language). Between 1987 and 1991, Xu Bing designed a "vocabulary" of 4,000 characters which look like Chinese but which are in fact illegible, entirely invented. He carved out each character in pear-wood type from which he hand-printed his "Book from the sky" or "Tianshu." One may be led to think that these characters are a long forgotten or indecipherable secret language. The characters vaguely resemble Tangut or Xixia script. The invention of such a convincing, official looking language speaks on many levels, but one meaning seems to stand out in particular for me: the authority of the text as form of symbolic power, regardless of how indecipherable, regardless of its truth value. [24]

Xul Solar Born in Buenos Aires in 1887, the only child of Emilio Schulz Rig, German from Letonia, and Augustina Solari, Italian from Genova. At sixteen he adopted the pseudonym Xul Solar using elements of his parents' surnames. He took interest in several subjects such as religion, philosophy, anthroposofia of Rudolf Stener, the Jewish Kabala, mythology, and astrology. He could speak and write six living languages, as well as Latin, Greek, and Sanskrit. This linguistic knowledge led him to create two languages, the "neocrilo" and "panlengua," conceptually similar to Esperanto. Xul Solar participated in a group called Martin Fierro during the twenties which helped to establish modernism in Argentina. Xul Solar produced hundreds of drawings and paintings; his work incorporates geometrically stylized human figures, architectural elements, flags, signs and symbols, numbers, letters, and hieroglyphics.

X A short-lived London quarterly review from the 1960s that included fiction, poetry, reproductions of paintings (e.g., Freud, Bacon, Auerbach), and essays on writing, architecture, and art. The review shunned avant-gardism in the name of "individualism, an interest in the soul, a respect for our revolutionary past, indifference to the topical label, a love of good painting and something rather painstaking which is not afraid of dullness."

Xeroxbook A canonical show/catalogue organized in 1968 by Seth Siegelaub and John Wendler in New York, comprised of a xeroxed catalogue with works by Carl Andre, Robert Barry, Joseph Kosuth, Sol LeWitt, and Robert Morris, among others. Considered to be one of the first conceptual art exhibitions.

X IS A WINDOW

(an exchange for two voices)

Voice I   But I don't understand why X means yes, this, right here, and at the same time, no, not this, not here.

Voice II   In time, X is this instant already gone; in space, it marks the way and bars entry in the same gesture. It is the window. The place where past and future meet.

Voice I   (*trying hard*) Do you mean that X is where we're at?

Voice II   You could say that. Everywhere and nowhere. The unknown. The mark and the substitution. The point of intersection. The place. The interface. (singing) The gesture that conveys all meanings. And none. You see (remembering the question) it cancels what it indicates and indicates what it cancels. It is the signature of ambiguity itself.

Voice I   (*enthusiastic*) Do you mean like the sign for pedestrian crossing and the mark for no exit?

Voice II   (*nodding*) X is the mark that embodies the twoness of existence. X is the window or moment between alternatives; it could mean either. A window distinguishes between self and other. You see through glass/you are barred from what you see. The glass shows and cancels at the same time. (explaining) People mark X's on windows because redundance is useful to perception. The X points out the access and the barrier so you don't hurt yourself. In that regard, it does what art does, it frames experience and makes it other. That is how self knows what self is. Or was. Or could be. It is immensely useful.

Voice I   Like an always up-to-date autobiography!

Voice II Exactly.

– Vera Frenkel, *The Big Book* [25]

... Let's say Nature, like femininity, is obsolete. She's simply a phantom who indolently twists the melancholic mirror of sex. Far into the rural distance, the horizon splays beneath her florid grip. In deep sleep, my ancestress tells me a story: 'Ontology is the luxury of the landed. Let's pretend you 'had' a land. Then you 'lost' it. Now fondly describe it. That is pastoral. Consider your homeland, like all utopia, obsolete. Your pining rhetoric points to obsolescence. The garden gate shuts firmly. Yet Liberty must remain throned in her posh gazebo. What can the poor Lady do? Beauty, Pride, Envy, the Bounteous Land, the Romance of Citizenship: these mawkish paradigms flesh out the nation, fard its empty gaze. What if, for your new suit, you chose to parade obsolescence? Make a parallel nation, an anagram of the Land. Annex Liberty, absorb her, and recode her: infuse her with your nasty optics. The anagram will surpass and delete the first world, yet, in all its elements, remain identical. Who can afford sincerity? It's an expensive monocle.'

– Lisa Robertson, *Xeclogue* [26]

SCRAPTURES: 17TH SEQUENCE

the religious man practises reversals

O
O

alpha
ahpla

omega
agemo

the reversed man practises religion

SUDDENLY I AM LIGHT   I   I   know(s

it is the face
it is the realization of the face

it is the facing
it is the realization of the facing

                    the split eyes

what the eye seizes as real is fractured again and again

          light

the eye's light

drifts away

diffused

by the mind's confusion

names and signatures

CHRIST become an X

X as the man signs who cannot write his name

as tho to be without a name were to take up the cross, so that a man who is part of the nameless, is part of the mass, carries the cross further, or is more weighed down by it

X—nameless

the reversal becomes complete

a cycle into the 30's

33
33

the trinity

X
saint reat
saint and

saint agnes who gave them a name

saint ranglehold

3

3

as the cock crowed   73

– bp nichol, *Gift: the Martyrology book(s) 7 &* [27]

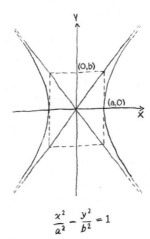

$$\frac{x^2}{a^2} - \frac{y^2}{b^2} = 1$$

other words [28]

x *n.* 1. The accelerator on a car (1950s). 2. An injection (1950s). 3. Marijuana or amphetamine.

x *v.* 1. To stop, eliminate. 2. **x out** U.S. Black. To discuss something as no longer important or relevant (1970s).

x-axis *n., pl.* **x-axes** 1. The horizontal axis of a two-dimensional Cartesian co-ordinate system. 2. One of three axes in a three-dimensional Cartesian co-ordinate system.

x-chair *n.* Also called scissors chair, Savonarola chair, or Dante chair. A chair supported by two crossed and curved supports either at the sides or at the back and front. Because of its basic simplicity, it is one of the oldest forms of chair or stool, its prototype reaching back to the 2nd millennium BC. Because of their scissor-like principle, they lent themselves to collapsible construction and thus appeared as folding stools in the early European Middle Ages.

X-chromosome *n.* The sex chromosome associated with female characteristics, occurring paired in the female and single in the male sex-chromosome pair. Compare Y-chromosome.

x-disease *n.* Hyperkeratosis. The hypertrophy of the horny layer of the skin.

x-height *n.* In printing, the height of lower-case *x*.

x-rated *adj. Informal.* 1. Having the rating X. 2. Explicit in the treatment of sex, indecency, violence; pornographic. Formerly said of film, given an x classification, suitable only for adults.

x-radiation *n.* 1. Treatment with or exposure to x-rays. 2. Radiation composed of x-rays.

x-ray *n.* 1. a. A relatively high-energy photon with wavelength in the approximate range from 0.05 angstroms to 100 angstroms. b. Usually plural. A stream of such photons, used for their penetrating power in radiography, radiology, radiotherapy, and research. Also called "Roentgen ray." [Translated from the German *X Strahlen* (so called because its exact nature was not known).] 2. **X-ray** A photograph taken with x-rays. 3. History. Discovered by Prof. W.C. Roentgen of Wurzburg in 1895, these rays were capable of passing through many substances impervious to light, and of affecting a sensitized plate, thus producing the shadowy effect of objects enclosed within opaque receptacles or bodies. Used most often in the medical field and at customs in airports.

X-ray source *n.* In astronomy, any of a class of cosmic objects that emit radiation at x-ray wavelength. Because the Earth's atmosphere absorbs x-rays very efficiently, x-ray telescopes and detectors must be carried high above it by spacecraft to observe objects that produce such electromagnetic radiation.

X-ray style *n.* A manner of depicting animals by drawing or painting the skeletal frame and internal organs, one of the characteristic styles of the art of prehistoric hunting cultures. The origin of the style can be traced to the Mesolithic art of northern Europe, where the earliest examples were found on fragments of bone in southern France dating from the late Magdalenian Period. Animals painted in the X-ray motif have also been discovered in the art of hunting cultures in northern Spain, Siberia, the Arctic Circle, North America, western New Guinea,

New Ireland, India, and Malaysia. It is found today primarily in the Aboriginal rock, cave, and bark paintings of eastern Arnhem Land, in northern Australia.

x-row *n.* The condemned cells of a prison (death row).

X-trisomy *n.* A sex chromosome disorder of human females, in which three X chromosomes are present, rather than the normal pair. It usually remains undetected because affected individuals appear normal, experience puberty, and are usually fertile. Statistical studies suggest a slightly increased frequency of mental disturbance, retardation, or both.

xanth-, xantho- Indicates the colour yellow.

xantha *n.* Any of many chloroplast mutations in various cereal species.

xanthate *n.* 1. A salt of xanthic (sulphocarethyllic) acid. 2. A compound of xanthic oxide (xanthine) with an alkali.

xanthein *n.* Also –ine. (Fremy and Cloez, 1854.) That part of the yellow colouring-matter of flowers which is soluble in water.

xanthelasma *n.* A disease which leaves yellowish or brownish patches on the skin; also called vitiligoidea.

Xanthicus *n.* The month of April in ancient Macedonia.

xanthine *n.* A yellowish-white purine base found in blood, urine, and some plants.

xanthinuria *n.* A rare inherited disorder of purine metabolism that results from a deficiency in the enzyme xanthine oxidase. It is not a serious condition, and many cases display no remarkable symptoms. Some people develop xanthine stones in their kidneys.

xanthochroi *n.* In Huxley's classification of different varieties of humans, a subdivision of the *Leiotrichi* or smooth-haired, having a yellow or light complexion and hair. *adj.* A *xanthochroid* individual.

xanthocyanopsy *n*. A form of colour-blindness in which yellow and blue are the only visible colours.

xanthodont, xanthodontous *adjs*. Having yellow teeth, as certain rodents.

xanthoma *n*. A skin disease characterized by nodular yellowish-orange patches, especially on the eyelids.

xanthometer *n*. An instrument for determining the colour of the sea or lake water by comparison with a scale of different-coloured solutions.

xanthommatin *n*. The brown ommochrome pigment of the compound eye of Drosophila.

xanthoparmelia *n*. A lichen genus, named for its yellow colour.

xanthophyll *n*. A yellow cartenoid pigment found with chlorophyll in green plants and in egg yolk.

xanthorrhoea *n*. A genus of Australian liliaceous plant, some species of which yield a yellow resin.

xanthospermous *adj*. Having yellow seeds.

xanthous *adj*. 1. Yellow. 2. Having light-brown or yellowish skin.

xanthoxylon *n*. A large and widely distributed genus of trees and shrubs, yielding various products, esp. pungent and aromatic drugs and condiments. It includes the North American Prickly Ash or Toothache-tree, the Chinese or Japanese Pepper, and the Prickly or West Indian Yellowwood.

Xe Symbol for xenon.

xebec *n*. A small three-masted Mediterranean vessel with both square and triangular sails, once commonly used by Arab corsairs.

xeme *n*. A bird of the genus *Xema*. A fork-tailed gull.

xen-, xeno- Indicates the presence of or a reference to that which is strange, foreign, or different. From the Greek *xenos* for guest, stranger.

xenacanthus *n.* A long-surviving but now extinct genus of freshwater sharks. It survived from the end of the Devonian Period, 345 million years ago, to about the end of the Triassic Period, 190 million years ago.

xenagogue *n.* One who conducts strangers; a guide.

xenelasy *n.* In Greek history, a measure at Sparta for the expulsion of foreigners.

xenia *n.* The effect on a hybrid plant produced by the transfer of pollen from one strain to the seed of a different strain.

xenial *adj.* Pertaining to the relation between host and guest.

xenization *n.* The act of sojourning as a stranger.

xenobiology *n.* 1. A branch of biology that deals with the search for and study of extraterrestrial living organisms. Also called exobiology or "astrobiology." 2. A branch of biology that deals with the effects of extraterrestrial space on living organisms.

xenobiotic *adj.* Denoting or involving a substance, usually a chemical compound, that is foreign to the body or to a particular ecological system.

xenocratic *adj.* To describe the doctrine of Xenocrates (396-314 BC), or someone subscribing to his ideals, one of these being a strict abstemiousness towards all earthly pleasures.

xenocryst *n.* A crystal foreign to the igneous rock in which it occurs.

xenodochy *n.* The entertainment of strangers.

xenogamy *n.* Cross-fertilization; the transfer of pollen from one plant to another; cross-pollination. *adj.* **xenoganous**

xenogenesis *n.* The supposed production of offspring markedly different from and showing no relationship to either of its parents. *adj.* **xenogenetic, xenogenic**

xenograft *n.* A tissue graft carried out between members of different species.

xenolith *n.* A rock fragment foreign to the igneous mass in which it occurs.

xenon *n.* A colourless, odourless, highly unreactive gaseous element found in minute quantities in the atmosphere, extracted commercially from liquefied air, and used in stroboscopic, bactericidal, and laser-pumping lamps. Atomic number 54, atomic weight 131.30, melting point –111.9°C, boiling point -107.1°C, density 5.887 grams per litre, specific gravity (liquid) 3.52 (-109°C).

xenophile *n.* Somebody attracted to foreign things, e.g. foreign manners, styles, people. *n.* **xenophilia**, *adj.* **xenophilic**

xenophobe *n.* A person unduly fearful or contemptuous of strangers or foreigners, especially as reflected in his/her political or cultural views. *n.* **xenophobia**, *adj.* **xenophobic**

xenotransplantation *n.* Transplantation of cells or organs from one species into those of another species, especially the use of pig cells and organs for transplantation into humans. This practice is still somewhat suspect due to the danger of illnesses crossing over from pigs to humans. Pigs are physiologically one of the closest animals to humans. Scientists initially cloned pigs thinking they could humanize cloned animals in order to produce transplant organs for humans. One of the most sublime instances of xenotransplantation was when human genetic material was grafted onto the back of a mouse; on this mouse there grew a human ear.

xer-, xero- Indicates dryness. From the Greek *xeros*, dry.

xeric *adj.* Of, characterized by, or adapted to an extremely dry habitat.

xeriscaping *n.* Dry-land gardening.

xeroderma *n.* Also **xerodermia**. Abnormal dryness of the skin.

xeroderma pigmentosum *n.* A group of hereditary diseases inherited as autosomal recessives in which the skin is extremely sensitive to sunlight or ultraviolet light, and death is usually due to skin cancer.

xerography *n.* A dry photographic or photocopying process in which a negative image formed by resinous powder on an electrically charged plate is electrically transferred to and thermally fixed as positive on paper or other copying surface. *adj.* **xerographic**, *n.* **xerographer**

xerophilous *adj.* Flourishing in or able to withstand a dry, hot environment.

xerophthelmia *n.* Extreme dryness of the conjunctiva, thought to result from vitamin A deficiency.

xerophyte *n.* A plant that grows in and is adapted to an environment deficient in moisture. *adj.* **xerophytic**, *adv.* **xerophytically**

xerosere *n.* A sequence of ecological communities beginning in a dry area.

xerosis *n.* 1. Abnormal dryness, especially of the skin, conjunctiva, or mucous membranes. 2. The normal evolutionary sclerosis of ageing tissue.

Xerox *n.* A sheet of paper printed through a photocopy machine. *v.* To print paper using a photocopy machine: *to xerox.*

Xerox queen *n.* *(1960s) U.S. gay.* A man who prefers all his sexual partners to resemble each other.

xesturgy *n.* The process of polishing.

Xg blood group *n.* A blood group defined by an antigen controlled by a gene located distally on the short arm of the human X chromosome.

xi *n.* 1. The 14th letter in the Greek alphabet, written Ξ. Transliterated in English as *X, x.* 2. Symbol. Physics. Either of two subatomic particles in the baryon family.

xilinious *adj.* Made of cotton.

xiphi-, xipho- Indicates sword.

xiphias *n.* A swordfish.

xiphisternum *n., pl.* –na. The posterior and smallest of the three divisions of the sternum. Also called "xiphoid process."

xiphoid *adj.* 1. Having the shape of sword. 2. Of or pertaining to the xiphisternum.

xiphophagus *n.* Conjoined twins united by a band extending downwards from the xiphoid cartilage. Also called Siamese twins, after Cheng and Eng, who were in fact xiphophagus.

Xiphophorus maculatus *n.* The platyfish, and *X. helleri,* the swordtail.

xiphosuran *n.* Any arthropod of the order Xiphosura, which includes the horseshoe crab and many other extinct forms. *adj.* Of or belonging to the order Xiphosura. From New Latin, *Xiphosura,* "sword-like ones."

X linkage *n.* The presence of a gene located on the X chromosome; usually termed "sex-link traits."

Xmas *n. Informal.* Christmas. From the Greek letter *X,* transliterated as *Kh* and representing Greek *Khristos,* Christ.

xoanon *n., pl.* **xoana.** A primitive rudely carved image or statue (originally made of wood), esp. of a deity.

xonotlite *n.* A hard massive hydrated silicate of calcium.

xu *n., pl.* **xu.** A coin equal to 1/100 of the dong, the monetary unit of North Vietnam.

xyl-, xylo- Indicates 1. Wood. 2. Xylene.

xylan *n.* A yellow, gummy pentosan found in plant cell walls and yielding xylose upon hydrolysis.

xylem *n.* The supporting and water-conducting tissue of vascular plants, consisting primarily of tracheids and vessels; woody tissue.

xylene *n.* 1. Any of three flammable isomeric hydrocarbons obtained from wood and coal tar. Also called "xylol." 2. A mixture of these isomers used as a solvent in making lacquers and rubber cement and as an aviation fuel.

xylidine *n.* 1. Any of six toxic isomers derived from xylene, used chiefly as dye intermediates. 2. Any of various mixtures of these isomers.

xyliglycon *n.* A carob- or locust-tree.

xylograph *n.* 1. An engraving on wood. 2. An impression from a wood block. *tr.v.* **xylographed, -graphing, -graphs.** To print from a wood engraving. *n.* **xylographer**

xylography *n.* 1. Wood engraving, especially of an early period. 2. The art of printing texts or illustrations, sometimes with colour, from wood blocks, as distinct from typography. *adj.* **xylographic,** *adv.* **xylographically**

xyloid *adj.* Of or similar to wood.

xylonite *n.* Another name for celluloid.

xylophagus *adj.* Feeding on wood, as certain insects.

xylophone *n.* A musical percussion instrument consisting of a mounted row of wooden bars graduated in length to sound a chromatic scale, played with two small mallets. *n.* **xylophonist**

xylose *n.* A white crystalline aldose sugar used in dyeing, tanning, and in diabetic diets. Also called "wood sugar."

xylotomy *n.* The preparation of sections of wood for microscopic study.

xyster *n.* A surgical instrument for scraping bones. From the Greek *xuster*, scraper, from *xuein*, to scrape.

xystra *n.* A currycomb (a comb for grooming horses).

xystus *n.* Among the ancient Greeks, a long covered portico or court used for athletic exercises. Among the ancient Romans, an open colonnade or walk, planted with trees, used for conversation or recreation.

All the alternatives; what is exchangeable;
all that is exterior to "I" or the self.

xeno- [29]

FROM A WESTERN HISTORICAL PERSPECTIVE

Xamaniqinqu Mayan god of the north.

Xavante Also Shavante. Brazilian Indian group speaking Xavante, a language of the Macro-Ge language family. Numbering about 3,000, they live in the southeastern corner of Mato Grosso state, between the Rio das Mortes and the Araguaia River. At one time they lived along the Tocantins River in Goias state, but pressure from Brazilian settlers in the 1840s forced the Xavante to move. They successfully defended their new territory against outsiders and lived in relative isolation until the 1930s when they gained notoriety in the wake of their resistance to the wave of settlers and government agents who were trying to bring central Brazil into the mainstream of Brazilian culture and economy. Traditionally they were nomadic hunters and gatherers who lived in temporary horseshoe-shaped villages on the savannah and cultivated corn, beans, and pumpkins. They hunted tapir, deer, wild pigs, and birds, and gathered roots, nuts, and honey.

Xbalanque One of the mythic twins that were grandchildren to the first human Mayan ancestors.

Xcalumkin A site of ancient hieroglyphs in Central America.

Xcosmil A site in the Yucatan where Puuc cave paintings can be found.

It is a small cave comprising a single room with a collection of twelve petroglyphs, consisting mostly of small frontal faces with circular eyes and mouth, ladder-like designs, and arabesques. One painting shows a "Kan" cross.

Xecotcovach A demon bird in Mayan mythology. It devoured the eyes of the first "failed" humans.

Xelas Also named Temaukl. The supreme being/creator of the tribes of Tierra del Fuego (the Ona, Yahgan, and Alacaluf Indians), living on the islands off Cape Horn, at the southern tip of the world.

Xevioso For the Fon people of Africa, the god of thunder.

Xhaaydla Gwaayaay Also Haida Gwaii. Literally means "Islands of the Boundary between Worlds." The Xhaaydla are a First Nations people from the "Queen Charlotte Islands," B.C. and southern tip of "Prince of Wales Island," Alaska, who speak Xhaaydla, believed to be a language isolate. As well as a unified language, the Xhaaydla share social, kinship, and inheritance systems in common but are divided into two major moieties, assigned at birth, based on maternal affiliation. Each moity in turn consists of many local lineages. The Xhaaydla economy was traditionally based on fishing and hunting. They are known for their skillful woodworking, particularly in the carving of canoes and totem poles. Xhaaydla potlatches, the ceremonial distribution of goods, were held to uphold and legitimize political rank or social status. Potlatches were also held to mark such events as house building, totem pole raising, funerals, as well as for revenge and face saving.

Xhosa Also Xosa. Means "The Angry Men" in Khoi language. One of the Bantu people of the Cape of Good Hope Province, South Africa. Also known as the Southern or Cape Nguni, they are composed of numerous groups of people concentrated mainly in the previous Transkei, Ciskei, and Eastern Cape regions. Xhosa is a Bantu language akin to Zulu. As with other African languages, it is a tonal language. The sound system of Xhosa contains three types of click sounds borrowed from the neighbouring Khoisan languages. In the late 18th and the 19th centuries, a series of conflicts known as the Kaffir Wars engaged the Xhosa against the European settlers in the eastern frontier region of Cape Colony. The Xhosa had been driven southward by overpopulation and land shortage, and encountered Cape colonists moving northward in search of farmland. The conflict lasted a century, but eventually the Xhosa were defeated. With the abolition of apartheid, Transkei and Ciskei became part of Eastern Cape province in 1994 after having been administered as a non-independent Black state in 1959. The Xhosa are agriculturalists who keep some cattle. They are organized into patrilineal clans, each associated with a tribe or chiefdom.

Xian In the Book of Zhuang Zi, a Daoist text from the 4th century BC, Xian is an immortal hermit who has skin like ice, lives on wind and dew, climbs clouds and mist, rides a dragon, and "wanders beyond the four seas." He protects creatures from disease and ensures good harvests. There are three categories of Xian: the celestial, terrestrial, and mountain/forest immortals.

Xi Wang Mu "Queen Mother of the West." In the Daoist mythology of China, queen of the immortals in charge of female genies who dwell in a fairy land called Hsi Hua. Her popularity has obscured Mu Kung, her counterpart and husband, a prince who watches over males in Tung Hua paradise. Tradition describes the queen as a former mountain spirit transformed from a quasi-human with a leopard's tail and tiger's teeth into a beautiful woman. Her fairyland garden was filled with rare flowers, extraordinary birds, and the flat peach of immortality.

Xibalba Name of the underworld in Quiché Maya mythology.

Xicaque Also Jicaque Indians, of Honduras.

Xiloj, Andres A contemporary Quiché Maya daykeeper and head of his patrilineage (helped with the recent translation of the *Popol Vuh* into English in 1985).

Xilonen Among the Aztecs, she is the goddess of maize, a fertility goddess, and protector of the home.

Xinca A group of about 10,000 Indians living in southern Guatemala along the Rio de los Esclavos, including most of the regions of Santa Rosa and Jutiapa.

Xingu The collective name of the tribes of the Alto Xingu from the Amazon Basin.

Xiongnu A nomadic pastoral people who, at the end of the 3rd century BC, formed a great tribal league that was able to dominate much of Central Asia for more than 500 years. China's wars against the Xiongnu led to the Chinese exploration and conquest of much of Central Asia.

Xipe Itzpapalotl Also named Camaxtle. An agricultural or star goddess.

Xipe Totec "Our Lord of the Flayed One." A pre-Columbian Mexican god of spring and of new vegetation. He was also patron of goldsmiths. As a symbol of new vegetation, Xipe Totec wore the skin of a human victim. His statues and stone masks always depict him wearing a freshly flayed skin.

Xipibo Andean Indians. See Shipibo.

Xiu An ancestral lineage of the ruling elite of the postclassic period, depicted as the limbs and flowers on the yaxche tree, seen growing from the loins of the lord Hun Uitzil Chac or as emerging from the mouth of a mountain cave. The yaxche tree protected the souls of the ancestral lineage.

Xiuhtecuhtli Aztec god of fire, thought to be the creator of all life.

Xkukican A cave in the Yucatan that has a collection of positive and negative handprints.

Xochicalco Ancient Toltec city known for its impressive ruins. Located on the top of a large hill and parts of surrounding hills near Cuernavaca, Mexico.

Xochimilco Built on the site of a pre-Columbian town. Famous for its *chinampas*, or floating gardens. Rafts were constructed by the native population on Lake Xochimilco, covered with soil, and fruits, vegetables, and flowers were cultivated. In time the rafts took root and became islands.

Xochipilli Aztec god of flowers, sport, dance, games, beauty, love, and youth. Husband of the eternally young Xochiquetzal.

Xochiquetzal Nahuatl for "Precious Feather Flower." She is a flower deity, patroness of unmarried women and of weavers, guardian of childbirth and new mothers. She is associated with flowers and plants and, in myth, came from Tamoanchan, the verdant paradise of the west.

Xochitel In Toltec and Aztec belief, a goddess and creator of Pulque, an intoxicating drink.

Xolata Also Choroti Indians, from South Bolivia.

Xolotl Aztec god of monsters, magicians, twins, the game play-ball, and of double ears of maize. Also dispenser of bad luck.

Xoquinoe Also Lacandon. Native Indians from Chiapas/Guatemala. As of the early 1980s, numbering slightly over 250 people.

!Xoo A language spoken by widely scattered groups of San (known as the Southern Bushman) living in southwestern Botswana and a small area of eastern Namibia. There are approximately 2,000 speakers. It is a tonal language that uses a system of clicks.

Xowalaci In one of the creation myths of the Joshua Indians of Oregon, Xowalaci was the creator who sat in the sweat house on the water. His friend sat outside and watched for land. When land struck the sweat house, Xowalaci smoked a pipe, blew the smoke on the land, and there, flowers and grass began to grow. Smoking tobacco also made the first human being appear – a woman.

Xquiq Mayan creator mother. Mother of Hunahpu and Xbananque.

Xuanantunich Mayan site in Belize.

Xuthus In Greek mythology, the son of Hellen, king of Phthia, and of the nymph Ortheis.

Xyatil A cave in the Quintana Roo of Mexico where one can find a black drawing of a frontal face.

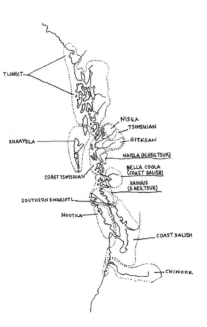

TLINGIT

NISKA
TSIMSHIAN
GITKSAN

XHAAYDLA

HAISLA (N.HEILTSUK)

BELLA COOLA
(COAST SALISH)

COAST TSIMSHIAN

XAIHAIS
(S.HEILTSUK)

SOUTHERN KWAKIUTL

NOOTKA

COAST SALISH

CHINOOK

"Since individual markings reveal the particularities of the mind of those who write, the national markings should permit to a certain extent researches into the particularities of the collective mind of peoples." [30]

In the translation of certain foreign, indiginous languages into our alphabet, x is often used to fill in for the sounds *sh, k,* and *ch* (as in Scottish lo*ch*). It is my theory that the x serves as an exoticizing signifier. Hence, the above quotation should not be taken literally. The use of x in its attachment to "others" reflects, rather, the particularities, the projective violence/fear, of the collective mind of European colonizers. Not a will to understand the other, but to project prejudice, power, ownership, onto the other. The letter x is a form of symbolic investiture, part of the logic behind the distribution of linguistic capital. One literary example of the use of the letter x within the colonial imaginary is that of Edgar Rice Burroughs in his books *Tarzan the Untamed* (the imaginary Xujan Kingdom, a walled city in Africa inhabited by a tribe of madmen who revere parrots) and *Return to Pellucidar* (Pellucidar being the underground continent in the southwest corner of which one finds Xexotland, a country of yellow-skinned Xexots). A counter argument to this theory of the use of x to exoticize, is the use of x by indigenous or First Nations groups as a means to distinguish their written phonetic identity from that inscribed by colonizers (e.g., the shift from Haida to Xhaaydla).

Logo-anglicized Chinese language: writes *x* (or *hs*) but is pronounced *sh*.

Logo-iberianized Maya, Xavante, Xingu, or Nahuatl language: writes *x* but is pronounced *sh*.

Logo-anglicized Xhosa language: writes *x* but is pronounced *k*.

Logo-anglicized Salish language: writes *x* but is pronounced *k* or *ch* as in German *buch*.

Logo-anglicized Haida Gwaii (Xhaaydla Gwaayaay) language: writes *x* but is pronounced a voiceless velar, like Russian *x*, the Arabic *kha*, the *ch* in German *buch*; or it is palatal, like the *j* in Spanish or the *ch* in German i*ch*. [31]

Logo-anglicized !Xoo language: writes *x* but is an aspirate *k* (uvular fricative). *!* stands for a click consonant.

SOME CHINESE WORDS BEGINNING WITH X

Xi	west
Xia	gorge, strait
Xian	county, shire
Xiang	village
Xiao	little
Xin	new
Xu	island

Some !xoo words beginning with x

(*preceded by a click consonant*) [32]

// xa.a	men
⊙ xaa	older brother
! xai	clothing
⊙ xoo	to walk swiftly
/ xaa	to dance
! xaa	to travel far
// xaa	to scrape

Some Salish (Bella Coola) words beginning with voiceless fricative phoneme x (palato-velar), x° (velar rounded), x̄ (uvular), x̄° (uvular rounded) [33]

xm	to break something
xmanwas	guardian spirit
xnas	woman
xli	penis
xil	to gnaw at a bone
x°p	to let go, put down
x°c	to demolish, take apart, break down
x̄m	to bite
x̄m-lx	dead tree

x̄s	fat
x̄lam-an-ta	cave
x̄°alt	to snore
x̄°is-m	to play, joke
x̄°uq	to scratch, rasp, file

SOME HAIDA WORDS BEGINNING WITH X [34]

Xhaaydla Gwaayaay (Haida Gwaii)
the islands on the boundary between worlds

Xhuuya	raven
xha	dog
xhaatgha	father
xhat	woman's father; also grave-post
xhel	hole
xhiihlsuu	heart

SOME XOLATA WORDS BEGINNING WITH X (CHOROTI)

xaman	north; praying mantis
xilal	man; manchild
xu'tan	end of the world

Nahuatl (Aztec)

xopancuicatl poetry; "a celebration of life and cyclical time: the poem and the poet become a plant that grows with the poem; the plant becomes the fibers of the book in which the poem is painted...."
(Eliot Weinberger) [35]

"If I am right in urging the overthrow of the Aryan Model and its replacement by the Revised Ancient one, it will be necessary not only to rethink the fundamental bases of 'Western Civilization' but also to recognize the penetration of racism and 'continental chauvinism' into all our historiography, or philosophy of writing history. The Ancient model had no major 'internal' deficiencies, or weaknesses in explanatory power. It was overthrown for external reasons. For 18th- and 19th-century Romantics and racists it was simply intolerable for Greece, which was seen not merely as the epitome of Europe but also as its pure childhood, to have been the result of the mixture of native Europeans and colonizing Africans and Semites. Therefore the Ancient Model had to be overthrown and replaced by something more acceptable." [36]

Martin Bernal's book *Black Athena* places Africa and the Near East not in the periphery but at the centre of Western historical discourse on the origins of our language. The European 19th-century fascination with India was based on the notion of Aryan ties between India and Europe, for instance with the notion of *the* original Western language being Indo-European (and later, with the use of the swastika as a symbol of purity in National Socialist culture). The lack of attention to Middle Eastern and African cultures was founded on racism, raising its ugly head with the birth of extreme forms of nationalism in light of the Napoleonic conquest at the end of the 18th century, increased trade and transportation, and cultural Romanticism. *Black Athena* questions the fabricated foundations of Western knowledge on

an Aryan model by tracing back Greek culture and language to its African and Semitic origins. According to Edward Said, because all knowledge is interested, all knowledge is framed, constructed. All Western thought reflects varying degrees of colonial discourse. After all, diffusion of language and culture occurred through conquest and trade. The 19th-century view held by European archaeologists, classicists, and philologists was that Greece was a self-generated culture, of pure origin, a non-Indo-European-speaking pre-Hellenic people who were later influenced linguistically by Kurgan Culture, originating north of the Black Sea (the "birthplace" of Indo-European language), that in turn influenced all of European culture. This was a rewriting of history. Before the 19th century, the Ancient Model held that Phoenicians and Egyptians had influenced Greek culture through migration and colonization. Bernal relegitimizes the Ancient Model of "origins," bringing Egyptian and Semitic culture back into service: the acknowledgment of Phoenician conquest of certain parts of Greece. He thus unmasks the racist cycle of seeing Africa and the Near East as objects of knowledge rather than as a source of Western thought and culture.

The shift from African/Semitic culture to Indian and a self-sufficient Greece, of course, came not from archaeological evidence but from the "discovery" of an Indo-European source of all Aryan languages. This is very much in keeping with racist scientific/positivist theories arising in the 19th century. Bernal's argument in favour of the Afroasiatic influences on Greece before that of Indo-European, or rather as a mixture of Afroasiatic and Indo-Hittite influence, created by the rift between cultural migration by land and by sea, shifts the notion of an *Urheimat* away from the north, toward the south. The whole issue of origins and of nationalist purity based on homeland is called into question in light of such a retracing of influences back to some mythic site (Ethiopia or the Ukraine/Caucasus). What becomes one's roots, one's homeland, is the result of conquest, of power struggles, of getting the upper hand, all of which is highly arbitrary. Having one's identity depend on the conqueror seems quite absurd.

But then subjectivity has always been constructed through the other. Lacan tells us that the *unconscious is the discourse of the Other.* Desire and subjectivity are constructed through identification with the other. During child development, primary thoughts and actions are repressed through contact with an other. In order to preserve oneself from conflict and to ensure satisfaction from the other one must keep certain traumatic thoughts repressed. One learns from the start that it is in one's interest to construct one's identity on the basis of the other mimetically. Conformity to symbolic power structures is the key to self-preservation. The ego is constructed in an external, object-oriented world filled with competing others. The subject is presented with the question of his/her existence: "What am I there?" (that which shall come into being outside "myself"). The question that one asks of the other in this process of construction is: "What do you want from me?" In philosophy, this concept of subjecthood can be traced back to Hegelian notions of a master/slave dialectic, which was based on the Platonic discourses, which in turn was much inspired by Egyptian culture and its caste system. The master/slave dialectic, found at the heart of the individual through the formation of the ego and the construction of desire, points to the very foundation of language. According to Lacan, human beings can have no access to language without first having traversed the imaginary (through seeing oneself as other) and the symbolic phase (of acknowledging that what one desires is dependent on the Other; what one desires is also what the Other desires). The movement between *fort/da* in games of occultation, the here/there or fleeting presence/absence of all things, is inscribed in language as a perpetual desire to make present an absence, to revisit or retrieve the "original" object of desire, now lost or absent, which leads to the idea of an "original" trauma, an "originary" trace of violence.

The swastika or swastica 卍 is an ancient cosmic or religious symbol. A Greek cross with arms bent at right angles, all rotating in the same direction. Usually clockwise but also counter. It signals good luck or prosperity.

The word is from the Sanskrit *svastika*, meaning "conducive to well-being." As a symbol it is found used in different parts of the world, in ancient and modern times. It was a favourite symbol on ancient Mesopotamian coinage. The symbol appears in early Christian and Byzantine art, known as the gammadion cross, or *crux gammata*, because it could be constructed from four Greek gammas. It has been found in South and Central America (the Maya) and in North America (principally the Navajo). It was used in Scandinavia as a sign for the hammer of Thor.

The swastika is still used today in India as an auspicious symbol of Hindus, Buddhists, and Jainas. The Hindus (and Jainas) use the swastika to mark the opening of pages of their account books, thresholds of doors, and offerings. The right-hand swastika (clockwise) is a solar symbol and the left-hand symbol often stands for night, the terrifying goddess Kali, and magical practices. For the Jainas, it is the emblem of the seventh Tirthankara and is said to remind the worshipper of the four possible places of rebirth (animal/plant world, hell, Earth, or the spirit world). For Buddhists, the swastika symbolizes the feet, or footprints, of the Buddha. It is often placed at the beginning and end of inscriptions, and modern Tibetan Buddhists use it as a decoration on clothing. With the spread of Buddhism it passed into the iconography of China and Japan, symbolizing abundance, long life, prosperity, plurality.

In 1910 Guido von List, a poet and nationalist ideologist, suggested the swastika (rotation clockwise ᛋ) be used as a symbol for all anti-Semitic organizations. When the National Socialist Party was formed in 1919, it adopted the symbol. A black swastika within a white circle on a red field became the national flag of Germany on September 15, 1935. The use of this flag/symbol ended at the end of World War II, when the Germans surrendered. The swastika is still used in the West by neo-Nazi groups/skinheads as a symbol for white supremacy and xenophobia. They embrace racism toward all non-Caucasian groups and blame all economic hardships on immigrants. [37]

Who are you? You don't know. Don't tell me Negro. That's nothing. What were you before white man called you a Negro? And where were you? And what did you have? What was yours? What language did you speak then? What was your name? It couldn't have been Smith or Jones or Bush or Powell. That wasn't your name. They don't have those kind of names where you and I came from. No. What was your name? And why don't you now know what your name was then? Where did it go? Where did you lose it? Who took it, and how did he take it? What tongue did you speak? How did the man take your tongue? Where is your history? How did the man wipe out your history? What did the man do to make you as dumb as you are right now? [38]

– Malcolm X

In *King Leopold's Ghost,* Adam Hochschild describes how Henry Morton Stanley and his officers were able to convince all the chiefs in the territory surrounding the Congo River to sign their land over to Belgium's King Leopold in return for little more than a few items of luxurious clothing and alcohol. Chiefs could not read or write, let alone speak their foreign tongue. Unable to write their names, they were asked to mark an X on documents whose contents they were ignorant of. Within the documents they signed, it was stated that they promised to "give up to the said [International African] Association the sovereignty and all sovereign and otherwise, any works, improvements or expeditions which the said Association shall cause at any time to be carried out in any part of these territories…. All roads and waterways running through this country, the right of collecting tolls on the same, and all game, fishing, mining and forest rights, are to be the absolute property of the said Association." [39] In time, the same right hands that signed these documents with an X were being cut off by the thousands. These hands were preserved as evidence of the number of victims killed during the rubber terror that spread through the Congo rainforest.

xylo-

"The form of wood ... is altered if a table is made out of it. Nevertheless the table continues to be wood, an ordinary sensuous thing. But as soon as it emerges as a commodity, it changes into a thing which transcends sensuousness. It not only stands with its feet on the ground, but in relation to all other commodities, it stands on its head, and evolves out of its wooden brain, grotesque ideas, far more wonderful than if it were to begin dancing of its own free will." [40]

The sublime (e.g., a burning bush).

x-rated

"... the law is no longer regarded as dependent on the Good, but on the contrary, the Good itself is made to depend on the law. This means that the law no longer has its foundation in some higher principle from which it would derive its authority, but that it is self-grounded and valid solely by virtue of its own form.... Kant, by establishing THE LAW as an ultimate ground or principle, added an essential dimension to modern thought: the object of the law is by definition unknowable and elusive.... Clearly THE LAW, as defined by its pure form, without substance or object of any determination whatsoever, is such that no one knows nor can know what it is. It operates without making itself known. It defines a realm of transgression where one is already guilty, and where one oversteps the bounds without knowing what they are, as in the case of Oedipus. Even guilt and punishment do not tell us what the law is, but leave it in a state of indeterminacy equaled only by the extreme specificity of the punishment." [41]

In ancient Greece, the word pornography referred to a subcategory of "biography" – tales of the lives of courtesans. For the Greeks, sexual gratification was dependent on class. Only the virile elite partook as agents in the art of sex. The "other," whether slave, foreigner, young boy, or woman, was the object of sexual desire (or humiliation) in their capacity as underdogs.

In the history of Western modern pornographic writing (from the late Renaissance forward), the narrator was virtually always a woman – often a literary whore – even though it was men's pens and penises actually calling the shots: men writing for other men. Male sexuality was obscured by the male gaze onto the female body, which was depicted in great detail, often with women having sex together. This had much to do with men's fear of contemplating their own sexuality – perhaps the fear of homosexuality as socially reprehensible under Christian law. Of course it was also a way of assuring that women would be excluded from being autonomous desiring subjects, thus keeping them in their dual roles as virgin/whore or mother/whore. Pornography, as the explicit depiction of sexual organs and sexual acts in view of arousal, was not a distinct category unto itself until the end of the 18th century, around the time of the French Revolution. For example, the meaning of the word pornography shifted completely between 1769, when Restif de la Bretonne used *pornographe* to mean writing about prostitution, and 1806, when Peignot's *Dictionnaire* used pornography to refer to writing that contravened social order and morality.

Pornography as a genre and sexuality as a category of the self began to emerge at the same time as modernity: the growth of cities, the rise of widespread property ownership and civil individualism, the invention of printing, the Scientific Revolution, the use of taxonomies and categories, the construction of the great humanist institutions (the university, prison, hospital, museum, etc.), the "birth" of the novel, the separation of life into public and private realms, a new materialist, liberal strain guiding the thought and imagination of the educated elite. This period also saw the emergence of a new conception of Law as existing independently of the Good. Law and civil duty was separated from the existence of a knowable morality. Imprisoned within the phenomenological, humans had to conduct themselves through the idea of being guilty before a Law that existed outside any knowledge of a necessary transcendental good. Because transgression cannot exist without law, pornography could be understood as a way of questioning the foundations of morality, law, and justice as carried out by church and state. The increase in production and investment in pornographic pleasures usually signaled a general crisis in authority, as during moments of historical rupture and social upheaval (e.g., the Reformation, the French Revolution, the late 1960s). Pornography has always contributed to the discourse of identity around the notion of *difference*. As a result pornography has almost always been misleadingly defined by those whose interest it is to regulate or even thwart difference.

Pietro Aretino's *Ragionamenti* and his *Sonnets* are considered the first modern instances of literary pornography, dating from the early sixteenth century. Erotic engravings accompanied these works. The *Ragionamenti* popularized the satirical and "realistic" dialogues between a young innocent woman and a more mature experienced woman. Pornography evolved with printing and started to become a recognizable genre with the birth of the novel in the 17th century (around the time of *Don Quixote*). Pornographic writing was dominated by the French, beginning with *L'Academie des dames* and *L'Ecole des filles* in the 17th century, and in the 18th with *Histoire de Dom Bougre*, *Thérèse philosophe*, *Les Bijoux indiscrets/Jacques le fataliste/La Religieuse* (Diderot), *Les Liaisons dangereuses* (Laclos), *Ode à Priape* (Piron), etc. Between the 1740s and the 1790s, pornography became increasingly political in France. It reached new heights at the beginning of the French Revolution with the Marquis de Sade's cataloguing of all manner of sexual perversions: sodomy, incest, rape, torture, etc.

With the accumulation of materialist knowledge about nature, anatomy, and the human body in the 18th century, and the primacy of physical mind over the concept of a transcendent soul or spirit, pornography grew to become a category guided by free thought (libertinism) and the valuing of nature and the senses as sources of knowledge. Philosophers applied sexuality to "the search for natural kinds" whereby sexuality was seen as an intrinsic force of nature. During this period, any explicit description of sexual organs and licentious acts was either influenced by scientific/philosophical discourse (naturalism and materialism) or based on a need to voice political/religious criticism. Scenes of debauchery were set in monasteries and palaces, revealing the hypocrisy of aristocratic privilege and of religious doxa. The production, use, and censorship of pornography was extremely complicated during the 18th century. On the one hand was the need to ritualize and regulate sex to contain the masses and prevent the spread of disease. On the other hand, expressions of sexual pleasure were seen to have emancipatory potential, and scientific research often revealed the benefits of a "healthy" sexual appetite.

At the same time, sexuality (and inadvertently its representation through pornography) was the result of an "intensification of the body" as produced by the many disciplinary institutions that were set up in view of classifying and controlling the human body. Foucault places this phenomenon at the close of the 18th century. Sexuality was produced by the very mechanisms that intended to control it. As the body was explored, measured, classified, and made into a thing, sexuality too was mapped and instrumentalized. The paradoxical nature of the "creation" of sexuality through the attempt to curb it can be illustrated by the attitude toward masturbation in the 18th and 19th centuries. With greater access to pornography and more discussion about what makes the body tick, masturbation was no doubt a worry for parents and religious groups. According to physicians, who took up the procreation cause like priests, onanism was the cause of a multitude of physical and mental ailments. Medical case studies took on a quasi-religious function as they outlined the decline of health caused by masturbation. Curing the patient of this activity took on the appearance of an exorcism of evil spirits.

Early pornography (16th-17th century) tended to be the domain of the elite. The democratization of pornographic material at the end of the 1790s erased most of what was ideologically subversive about pornography. Without the critical/political function or ideological context, pornography became an autonomous category, tending toward a display of anonymous bodies, of nameless anuses, cunts, cocks, and tits, pushing and pulling within arbitrary relationships of master/servant, voyeur/exhibitionist, etc. Or it tended toward "pornutopia," whereby all time-space coordinates were forfeited in the name of some ahistorical world of repeated sexual encounters, the endless combination of interchangeable bodies and parts. One thinks of de Sade's underground caverns as such a pornutopian site. But if all bodies and their parts were in fact interchangeable then class, gender, and racial differences would lose their meaning. This, of course, was not the case.

When pornography lost most of its political edge, sexual arousal became an aim in itself. It filled the streets and commercial strips with the same industrial logic as commodities. With the circulation of more capital and with more leisure time and commodity goods available thanks to industrialization, there was an increased blurring of class boundaries. Throughout the 19th century, with the growth of literacy, the spread of education, and the rise of the bourgeoisie, there was an increase in demand for pornographic material from the lower strata of society. The uses of photography, and later film, meant that pornographic representation was made even more life-like and accessible. The elite had always kept pornography under control in the name of scholarship, for there was no telling what kinds of acts of deprivation the working classes would be up to once exposed to sexually explicit material. Neither could urban, middle- to upper-middle-class women of this time period be exposed to such pornographic material. The danger of emancipation and rebellion by the working classes and women, and of unbridled non-family oriented sex, meant that the male elite censored pornography (for their own covert use). Instead they advanced shopping, pre-cinematic spectacles, and later, film, as healthy and moral pastimes. The result was a period of sexual conservatism and industrial/market growth in America and in Europe, coinciding with the concept of Victorian morality.

Women were denied sexuality while men were to keep it hidden from view (as photos, in brothels, etc.). Homosexuals were openly persecuted and books on birth control were banned. Bourgeois women remained confined to the private sphere, and yet there was a growing sex industry. Courtesans were still available, but there was another type of woman on public display, found on the commercial strip, the street prostitute.

Censorship ran rampant during the late 19th and early 20th centuries. Although hardly qualifying as "pornographic" by today's standards, Gustave Flaubert's *Madame Bovary* and D.H. Laurence's *Lady Chatterley's Lover* are two examples around which legal battles were waged against authors whose writings transgressed social norms (see **Index**). In the end, such censorship cases being fought out between publishers/authors and the law helped to publicize these works because it whetted readers' appetites for more transgressive genres, thus creating a new market for such books. After World War II, the veil of Victorian morality was torn away with the increase in scientific study of sexuality (Kinsey) and with a more "democratized" cultural pornography. Rather than weaken the structure of the nuclear family, it reinforced the existing sex and gender norms by eroticizing marriage and monogamy. Sexuality was commodified and found its place within the rules of capitalism. This became apparent with the emergence of *Playboy* in the 1950s and then of a saucier *Penthouse* and *Hustler* in the following decades. In the 1970s, many feminists began to protest the exploitation of women as objects of convenience for men. The result was an expansion of the market in the form of soft porn for women. But in most cases this did little more than reverse the voyeuristic roles of the gaze, and the market was limited because of laws against depicting erections. Feminist books, on the other hand, explored the notion of women's sexuality as multiple, extra-genital, and not dependent on dominant/subservient sex roles. Still other feminists became anti-porn activists, mistaking the commercial sex industry with the sexism that pre-exists in society as a whole.

The hard core industry developed in the early '70s in Denmark, Germany, and Sweden, often depicting mutually desiring agents (non-traditional gender roles) rather than normative heterosexual ones. As homosexuality became more and more accepted through increased activism in the '70s and '80s, the pornography industry further flourished. As a political statement on freedom from heterosexual and patriarchal constraints, sexuality was, again, something to be redefined and reproduced within the booming entertainment industry (through magazines, film, and video). Multiple encounters and all manners of sex, including such practices as fisting, sado-masochism, pissing, and shitting, were bracketed as political acts unto themselves, for gays, lesbians, and bisexuals were asserting their right to alternative lifestyles. Having access to pornographic writing, imagery, and other paraphernalia was a form of symbolic sanction. This politicization of sexual orientation was further complicated by the (continuing) AIDS epidemic when Christian fundamentalist factions waged a war against what they understood as the wages of sin: non-reproductive practices of sex were punished by God. Responsible preventative measures such as Dr. C. Everett Koop's brochure about AIDS, sent to every household in the U.S., were considered by puritans as little more than pornographic material meant to condone alternative lifestyles.

Up until the 19th century pornography had often been used to criticize the aristocracy and the church. In the latter half of the 20th century, as well as providing the means toward sexual gratification, pornography was used by homosexuals and bisexuals as a way to challenge the naturalization of heterosexual relations, a view reproduced within all social institutions. Robert Mapplethorpe's photographs are a case in point, and were also the target of a new round of censorship cases, this time brought against visual artists by Jesse Helms et al. Recently, more and more pornographic material has been produced by women in film, literature, and visual art and have been the site of controversy (e.g., *Baise Moi* by Virginie Despentes and Coralie Trin Thi, *La vie sexuelle de Catherine M.* by Catherine Millet, and Sarah Lucas' *Au Naturel*).

More nefarious intentions that stage flagrant instances of violence and victimization (as in child porn, abuse towards women, and snuff films) are banished to the realm of hardcore porn in this book, and are filed away and censored as X, that is, the unsayable, the monstrous. [42]

XVII. MARY PISSES ON THE COUNT

Mary said to the Count:

"I'm afraid of you! You're there in front of me like a bollard…."

He did not reply. Pierrot took hold of his cock: he was motionless.

"Go away," screamed Mary, "or I'll piss on you…."

She climbed onto the table and squatted.

"I'll be delighted if you do," replied the other.

His neck was inflexible. When he spoke, his chin moved.

Mary pissed.

Pierrot was wanking the Count, while a jet of urine slammed into his face: the count reddened and the urine drenched him. Pierrot wanked as he drank: the penis spat spunk onto the table and the dwarf trembled from head to toe (like a dog shaking gristle).

– George Bataille, *The Deadman* [43]

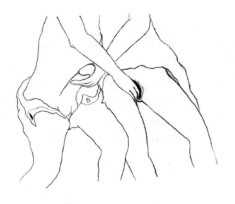

XX & XY (& X, XXX, XXY, XXXY, XYY, XYYY, XYYYY)

WHEN THE TRUTH IS IN GENES

Traditionally we have been taught that gender in humans is cut and dried. Male and female. This could be proven scientifically by analyzing biological sex. Humans normally have 46 chromosomes: 22 pairs of autosomes and a 23rd pair made up of two sex chromosomes, either two Xs or an X and a Y. If you had two such X's you were female and if you had an X and a Y you were male. The Y chromosome is extremely small compared to the X, and holds few genes, most of which are duplicates of genes lying on the X. This XY is an odd coupling. For whereas every chromosome is coupled with an identical chromosome in the other 22 pairs, the X has the choice of coupling with a Y. Y is a veritable stump of a chromosome. And it is more vulnerable to X-linked traits such as colour blindness, haemophilia, and fragile X syndrome (resulting in mental retardation).

Things get a little confusing, however, when you have female athletes who are tested and discover themselves to be genetically male XY, even though their outer apparatus is decidedly female. You have men who are XX and sterile even though they have penises. You have masculine women and feminine men, you have men who feel like women trapped in a male body, you have women who feel like men trapped

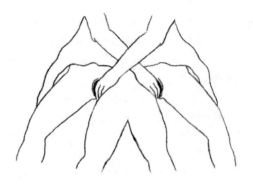

inside a female body. These people need a sex change. You have plenty of other grey areas. Some genders feel neuter, some people are asexual, some swing both ways; some sexes are born hermaphroditic, are operated on as infants, only later to find out that they would have preferred the other choice. The idea of a two-gendered species seems more and more absurd. You have theories that rationalize the fluidity of sexuality and gender as an evolutionary process, purporting evolutionary behaviour based on overpopulation, etc. Others call it genetic mutation.

In the first weeks of life, the human embryo is neither male nor female. It is externally impossible to distinguish a male from a female foetus. It is now considered common knowledge that until seven weeks of gestation, the two sexes are physiologically the same, and that the "default" body plan is always "female." The gonads are present and can either become testes or ovaries at this point. There is also a genital ridge which can either become a clitoris and labia or a penis and scrotum. Two primordial duct systems occur in all foetuses: the Mullerian duct that grows into the uterus, fallopian tubes, and vagina, and the Wolffian ducts that become seminal vesicles, the vas deferens, and epididymis. During the eighth week, if the foetus has a Y chromosome, a single gene located on the short arm of the Y chromosome, testis-determining factor (TDF), will trigger the gonads to turn into testes, which in turn produces male hormones like testosterone which in turn produces dihydrotestosterone. The testes also produce Mullerian inhibiting factor, which causes the feminine Mullerian ducts to atrophy and be absorbed by the body. The female foetus has no triggering mechanism as occurs in the Y chromosome. By the thirteenth week, her gonads begin to turn into ovaries and her Wolffian ducts shrivel up. It is important to remember that sex is much more a matter of hormones than of chromosomes. In fact, it has been proven that the hormone environment of the womb has more to do with

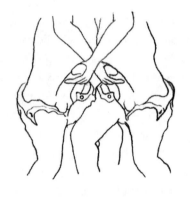

determining the sex, sexuality, or gender of the foetus than chromosomes.

There are cases where an XY foetus has "androgen insensitivity" such that "he" develops testes and testosterone but "his" body doesn't recognize the testosterone and the body goes the female route instead. The outer female genital characteristics develop, but the inner ones do not. Except for the presence of the testes, the child looks like a girl.

One in every 2,500 females has only a single X chromosome; this is called Turner's syndrome. These women look very feminine but have no developed ovaries.

Some women have an X and a Y but the Y, has no TDF gene, and therefore the women are much like those with Turner's syndrome, feminine but sterile.

Some males have two Xs, but the gene for TDF has migrated onto one of the X chromosomes. This causes the foetus to develop into a male body despite the female set of sex chromosomes.

Klinefelter's syndrome occurs in males who possess two Xs and one Y (XXY). These men tend to have small genitals, minimal sperm, and slight breast development. XXXY males have even more ambiguous genitals.

Females can have three Xs or males an extra Y (XYY) and still have "normal" sexual development. Males with an extra Y are decidedly more aggressive in behaviour. There is no such thing as a YY male. It is not genetically or humanly possible.

There is a newly discovered gene that is found on the X chromosome – DAX. In extremely rare cases, people are born XY but with two copies of the DAX gene on their X chromosome. These genetically male people develop into females sexually. This occurs because two DAX genes cancel out SRY, a male-defining gene on the Y chromosome.

Many geneticists see the relationship between X and Y chromosomes as an antagonistic one, their present configuration the result of evolution. Y is considered as being always on the defense, on the manipulative track, when it comes to survival. The Y chromosome is said to be, of all genes, the one that has most evolved over the millennia. Because it only occurs twenty-five percent of the time in bodies, as opposed to the X, which occurs seventy-five percent of the time, it has had to shed most of its genetic matter and maintain a highly specialized function. In his book *Genome*, Matt Ridley has gone so far as to hypothesize that humans evolved from apes in large part due to the Y chromosome's need to survive dominance and "manipulation" by X. Even intelligence is said to stem from this sexual gene conflict: "The notion that our brains grew big to help make tools or start fires on the savannah has long since lost favour. Instead, most evolutionists believe in the Machiavellian theory – that bigger brains were needed in an arms race between manipulation and resistance to manipulation. 'The phenomena we refer to as intelligence may be a by-product of intergenomic conflict between genes mediating offense, and defense in the context of language', write Rice and Holland." [44]

Xq28

A controversial theory emerged in 1993 regarding a "gay gene." According to Dean Hamer, there was a gene on the X chromosome (thus transmitted by the mother) that caused homosexuality in men. This study was of particular interest to such scientists as Simon LeVay who himself was gay, and wanted to research a gene that could possibly prove that being gay was an innate characteristic and not merely a lifestyle choice. In their research it was noticed that the hypothesized gene was carried on the female line: "If a man was gay, the most likely other member of the previous generation to be gay was not his father but his mother's brother." Hamer compared the genes of gay men and found that seventy-five percent of the time there was a common genetic marker on the tip of the long arm of the X chromosome, Xq28. However, this gene has never been found let alone decoded.

Another explanation for homosexuality is the presence of three active genes on the Y chromosome, H-Y minor histocompatibility antigens. It is uncertain what these genes do. They are not essential for the masculinization of the genitals, but it has been theorized as being instrumental to the masculinization of the psyche. What scientists have discovered is that men with one or more older brothers are much more likely to be gay than those with younger brothers or older sisters, etc. Each additional elder brother apparently increases the probability of being gay by about one-third. The rationale behind this observation is that the H-Y antigens produce an immune reaction in the mother during gestation. This immune reaction is said to increase with successive male pregnancies, with each new contact to Y chromosomes present in the womb. The H-Y antigens' function is supposedly to trigger the "masculinization" (or should we say, rather, the heterosexualization) of the brain in accordance with that of the genitals. A strong immune reaction against these antigen proteins on the part of the mother would be to prevent the masculinization of the brain. These "antibodies" produced by the mother increase in concentration with each new male birth. This apparently causes future males to be less "masculinized" cerebrally, and thus be more attracted to other males, less to females. [45]

These theories look for biologically innate reasons for homosexuality in order to counter social intolerance and paranoia (perhaps a paranoia of themselves being "infected" by such a "virus"). This is all very clever in theory but does nothing to analyze the symptoms of homophobia within the social economics of heterosexuality (e.g., family values). What would it mean for a masculinized brain to be attracted to another masculinized brain? What are these gendered genes and what qualifies them? What is innately masculine or feminine in terms of behaviour? What is innate and what is acquired? It is all anything but cut and dried, and the rationale behind scientific research into such areas remains stagnant and even deeply entrenched in prejudice, because it is based on the heterosexual yardstick of what constitutes "normal" behaviour. When the body comes to believe in what it plays at or performs by habit in day-to-day life, this is called "practical belief" (Bourdieu). There is a socially constructed fear of homosexuality to begin with and this is reproduced below the level of conscious behaviour within society. Homophobia and gender inequality are based not so much on humans' survival instincts, the fear by all citizens that family lineage will be cut short, that their particular cocktail of gene selection that has been developing for millennia, will suddenly be cut short in their particular instance; rather, homophobia is grounded in a network of ideological beliefs that have penetrated our social mythology from "above." The normalization of heterosexuality feeds into the capitalization of big business on the high consumption rate of competing families. As seen in recent advertising strategies, gay- and lesbian-oriented marketing strategies perpetuate "safe" stereotypes in view of the same goal: profit.

X-Files

Like the sound of a body bag being zipped up around an alien body, *The X-Files* resounds in our homes with what could only be characterized as a post-Cold War hangover. Behind every *X-Files* case lies some secret government experiment or program, some knowledge of extraterrestrial life kept hidden from the public. The paranormal, UFOS, conspiracy theories, secret scientific experiments involving genetic hybridization, all come together rather seamlessly in our "present moment," all the while hearkening back to a rather paranoid period in history that had supposedly just come to an end – 1947–1989.

In some ways, *The X-Files* does not seem to follow a postmodern formula. It avoids an overly cynical point of view. Its motto is "The truth is out there," suspending disbelief in the name of a higher purpose, a hidden universe of transcendent meaning. It often leaves you hanging by a thread. The conclusions of a show never completely resolve the trouble surrounding the appearance of paranormal activity. Instead the thread is picked up in the next episode, the thin lifeline of belief holding up to all scientific and rational pressure. Scully straddles the two worlds of the paranormal and the scientific community (see xenobiology), acting as the bridge of suspended disbelief that the viewer tends to relate to.

In some ways, however, the show is postmodern in terms of creating a serial universe of self-referentiality. No episode is ever quite self-sufficient, often alluding to previous episodes. *The X-Files* had a cult status, attracting a select "market niche" of avid viewers, a type of fan viewership that began with *Star Trek* and reached a new height with *Twin Peaks*. The *X-Files* also mixes genres – sci-fi, horror stories, noir undertones, FBI or detective scenarios, new-age "metaphysics" – all the right ingredients for a postmodern game in appropriation savvy. Allusions span '50s, '60s, and '70s TV viewing. A network era feel, without the flagrant family-values ethics of consumption rammed down your throat. Secret attractions are never consummated. The family with two kids and a house with a two-door garage never materializes between Mulder and Scully, is kept purgatorially on hold. There is a continual relapse into childhood wonder and fear of the bogeyman. A particular ideology insinuates itself furtively, appealing to an "educated" fan base.

And then there's the presence (or non-presence) of Vancouver, where the show was shot. A postmodern city in its own right, having begun to experience the big boom just around the transition period from Fordism to Flexible Accumulation (1973) and displaying its own symptoms as a city within the show itself. The noir elements tie in well, especially since one is not supposed to know that the filming actually takes place in Vancouver. The persistence of night, the suburban looking sites, a west coast look that makes visible the L.A. and *Twin Peaks* (Washington state) connection without actually spelling it out for you. The predominance of dark alleyways and cellars. Damp and humid. Capable of growing the most monstrous creatures. Without identity.

So ... 1947. Why this date in particular you might ask.

1947 signals the beginning of the Cold War period, the year Nixon first took office in Congress and the House Un-American Activities Commission (HUAC) began investigating communist infiltration in the media, the year of the first UFO sighting by civilian pilot Kenneth Arnold around Mount Rainier, of the Roswell crash, when the Jersey

Devil first appeared, when alien tissues were first collected by the government, and when the governments of the U.S., the Soviet Union, China, Germany, Britain, and France all secretly agreed to kill any alien life form they retrieved from a UFO crash. In September of that year, President Truman created the Majestic Twelve, a group of top-secret experts who were to investigate UFO events in Roswell.

The connections between UFO sightings, the paranormal, and Cold War politics are even more flagrant in certain episodes. In "Little Green Men," we witness a flashback of the alien abduction of Mulder's sister when they were children (the original impetus behind his dedication to the X-Files within the FBI). Just before the abduction happens, Mulder and his sister are arguing about what they want to watch on television. The viewer may notice that the TV shows Nixon during the Watergate scandal, when several minutes from one of Nixon's tapes has been discovered to be erased. The show makes an explicit connection between government cover-ups and alien sightings and abductions.

The X-Files weaves together all types of conspiracy theories: that alien phenomena might be a comical cover-up for government misbehaviour, that the military knows about alien life forms but hides this information from the public, that government agencies conduct secret genetic experiments that create mutant life forms. One is always left wondering: is the government collaborating with UFOs, or is it trying to fight/control them? In the end, the show refrains from passing any final judgement. This mythologizing of military investigations into UFO sightings maps Cold War politics over alien abduction theories. Communism was proof of one's un-Americanness during the HUAC investigations: "... earthly and unearthly monsters alike operated according to one principle: infiltration. Once inside the system, takeover was nearly inevitable. Only federal agents and brilliant scientists could exterminate the brutes." [46] In the absence of the Soviet enemy in 1993, the government is portrayed as fighting a metaphorical demon of the Cold War. Aliens. The genetic engineering and hybridization scenarios strike pretty close to home in the present. With the recent mapping of the human genome, the decision to clone humans and animals (the Raelians in particular), and the covert introduction of genetically modified foods on the market, one cannot help but be taken in by the feasibility of conspiracy, of all that controls and infiltrates the body unbeknownst to us. All seems to point more than ever at something rotten in the Law. The foundations of power are at this moment in the process of being buried deep within the very cellular structure of all living things.

X-Men

The original *X-Men* comic book was launched in 1963 by Marvel Comics under the editorship of Stan Lee. It is interesting to note that this was the year after the Cuban Missile Crisis when the U.S. and the former Soviet Union were on the brink of nuclear war. In many ways *X-Men* could be understood as a product of that growing fear of nuclear threat.

The new ingredient in the Marvel superheroes of the 1960s was a new type of irony, coupled with an anti-heroic stance in many of the characters – the hero with problems. The underlying concept of *X-Men* integrated doubt and irony in the relationships between characters, a distrust and suspicion in the fabric of their very relationship as a team. The X-Men were mutant teenagers, both male and female, who possessed extraordinary powers (hence the X), powers that set them apart from the rest of humanity. They are alienated from society. The appearance of such mutations is explained as being the result of increased radiation in the earth's atmosphere (caused by human manipulation of the elements? are mutants the by-product of Cold War nuclear testing?). Mutant powers lay dormant until the onset of puberty (much like the superpower drive of hormones turns adolescents to reckless death-defying feats of "heroism" and sexual promiscuity). A team of these young mutants are assembled around the wheelchair-bound middle-aged mutant leader, Professor Charles Xavier (Professor X). He is a telepath and runs a school for gifted (mutant) youth.

In many ways, this "high school" for the gifted could be perceived as a boot-camp-type institution where they were training for future instances of deadly combat. Because of their often disturbing appearance, they are shunned by society, even though they have sworn to protect the world from evil forces. A scenario where mutant teenagers were fated to be loathed and feared by society attracted adolescent sensibilities who were already plagued by feelings of isolation and alienation. Mutants had to hide their "real" identities in order to remain "at large." This situation also seems to point to the increased presence of paramilitary forces in the postwar period, especially in the U.S.

The original *X-Men* were comprised of Cyclops (whose eyes emitted death rays), Marvel Girl (able to move objects using telekinetic powers), Angel (could fly; had powerful wings), The Beast (gorilla strength, but erudite), and Iceman (reverse human torch; able to freeze anything). The comic ran for sixty-six issues, with reprinted material occupying *X-Men* 67-93. These teenaged superheroes were close-knit, often describing themselves as a family unit, working under the mentor/father-figure of Professor Xavier. The X-Men's arch-nemesis was Magneto, Master of Magnetism and chief of the "Brotherhood of Evil Mutants" – an organization that used mutant powers to dominate inferior homo sapiens.

There was a revival of *X-Men* comics in 1974 (*Giant-Size X-Men*), with writer Chris Claremont. The new series made the term "mutant" a household word. Angel, Beast, and Iceman were replaced by an international line-up, reflecting the new economic forces of globalization. Nightcrawler was a teleporting blue furry German elf circus freak, Colossus, a muscular Russian who could transform his body into living steel, Storm, an African Goddess with mutant power over the weather, Banshee, an Irish ex-villain with a sonic-scream, Thunderbird, an Apache with speed, agility, and tracking skills (who is soon killed off), and Wolverine, a psychopathic Canadian with unbreakable

bones and claws that could pop out of his knuckles. Cyclops was the only one to stay on from the former group, serving as Professor X's deputy and field commander. Marvel Girl comes back on the scene in later issues.

Through using an international line-up of superheroes, Marvel was hoping to attract a more international audience. The new *X-Men* was Marvel's most popular title and became even more so when the artwork was taken over by John Byrne, using a detailed cinematic style. Terry Austin was inker, and Glynis Wein did colouring. *X-Men* continued on until the late 1980s. The comic has been recently revived with the arrival of the *X-Men* movie in 2000.

Members were constantly coming and going, personalities remaining mercurial. Unresolved conflicts between the characters (reminiscent of repetitive family squabbles and conflicts) ran through the series, outlasting any individual plot-line, and became one of the main driving forces of the comic's development. This internal rivalry was essential to the team dynamic. The most far-reaching conflict remained the one between the team leader Cyclops and the newcomer Wolverine. Two entirely different views on superhero qualities formed the backbone of the tension between Cyclops and Wolverine, the American patriot versus the exiled Canadian. Another one of the main conflicts of *X-Men* was the problem of Colossus maintaining his strength when confronting the enemy, and of his being brainwashed and inadvertently turning against the team. The fact that Colossus was Russian is not accidental. The Cold War between Russia and America was foremost in people's minds. In *X-Men*, one also had to be wary of the Russian communist mentality.

The new *X-Men* was dominated by Colossus, Cyclops, and Wolverine; however, Storm, the African Goddess, also enjoyed a period as leader to the X-Men. She embodies the forces of mother nature and the exotic, but she also plays a quasi-maternal role within the X-Men family. She reconciles the conflicts between the male characters by playing a typically traditional female role.

The characters seem very bent on navel-gazing, and there is a need for self-help or group therapy in order to come to terms with their marginal status vis-à-vis society. So many of the episodes have to do with character analysis and self-improvement. The *X-Men* movie evinces this same preoccupation with character development, group relationships, and auto-analysis at the expense of plot. Overcoming the enemy goes hand in hand with overcoming the problems within (metaphorized by their mutations which give them power but also weakness – social and psychological). In the end, the comic strip seems to be more about lifestyle and egocentrism than anything else. It is a universe unto itself, a world of conflicting/competing mutants, divorced from any preoccupation with the human world. Being alienated from society, they seem in the end to have given up on society altogether. *X-Men* is characterized by a certain dystopian vision, a certain belatedness in its view of the future. [47]

Generation X

"'You must be Andrew,' he said, and he shook my hands like a Ford dealer. 'Come on upstairs. We'll have drinks. We'll talk,' he said.... And as we were walking toward the elevator, I could feel everyone in the office shooting jealousy rays at me. It was such a bad scene and I could just imagine everyone thinking 'who does he think he is?' I felt dishonest. Like I was coasting on my foreignness. I felt I was being excommunicated from the *shin jin rui* – that's what the Japanese newspapers call people like those kids in their twenties at the office – new human beings. It's hard to explain. We have the same group over here and it's just as large, but it doesn't have a name – an *X* generation – purposefully hiding itself. There's more space over here to hide in – to get lost in – to use as camouflage. You're not allowed to disappear in Japan.... It was then that he asked me what I thought the most valuable *thing* was that I owned ... So I said quite truthfully (and, it dawned on me, quite re*fresh*ingly), that I owned no *thing* of any value.... He reached in and pulled out what I could tell to be from the distance, a photograph – a black-and-white 1950s photo, like the shots they take at the scene of the crime.... It was a photo of Marilyn Monroe getting into a Checker cab, lifting up her dress, no underwear, and smooching at the photographer, presumably Mr. Takamichi in his stinger days.... Looking at it, I said to Mr. Takamichi, who was waiting expressionlessly for a reaction, "well, well," or some such drivel, but internally I was actually quite mortified that this photo, essentially only a cheesy paparazzi shot, unpublishable at that, was his most valued possession." [48]

Much has been written about Generation X since Douglas Coupland's book came out a decade ago. *Generation X* speaks to a white middle-class audience about the trials and tribulations of living in a post-boomer culture. The fashionable postmodern references are nostalgic beyond belief – they take part in a smug, post-capitalist irony. One revels in a completely post-historical fantasyland of trash and toxicity, convenience stores, strip malls, car culture, and suburban anomie. One is classified as little more than a demographic, or rather, psychographic tendency. Reality is not a given. It is generated. It is something that must be bought (into). To possess and be possessed by.

The above quotation is particularly telling. One of this generation's redeeming qualities is its sense of historical distance and cynicism. Perhaps stemming from that purgatorial feeling of having arrived too early or too late. The photograph that the business man pulls out of his safe for Andrew to see is considered his most valued possession. For the X-er, this is the litmus test that, once immersed in the sludge of postwar media culture, reveals the soullessness of the boomer generation that has traded human ideals for spectacle value. The hope is that one will not mistake such pap as the philosophical letter that lies deep within the individual, only to be disclosed at the moment of death (Coupland's idea, after Rilke). The meeting between Japanese businessman and disillusioned North American is a tense and beautiful one, but the novel's protagonist overlooks the cultural difference that gives the incident its poignancy (think of the U.S.'s unilateral occupation of Japan, the price it had to pay for its postwar economic prosperity). The pornographic photo of Marilyn Monroe symbolizes perhaps the installation of a government regime of institutional corruption within Japan, enforced by the United States up until the early '90s. The fact that it is a feminine American icon displaying her most private parts, and that such a photograph is kept in one's safe, reverses the role of possession, reverses the "feminized" role projected onto the Japanese.

Generation X is most often used as a derogatory term for those born in the '60s and '70s who became a synonym for slackerdom, the aimless, postmodern angst of a generation born with nothing left to rebel against, and no meaningful fulltime jobs to fill. The boomers had made their point, been in the TV spotlight, and then quickly lost their utopian illusions once they saw how ineffectual their tactics were against the military-entertainment machine. But there was this historical fulcrum on which they continued to teeter-totter through life. This anchor. This safety-net. What did we get? An even more marketable, expendable youth. The oil embargo of 1973 was the first alarm signaling that the grand vision of a utopia was over. Free market capitalism beginning in 1980 followed closely on its heels.

To have had it that easy, to have basked in the cult of youth and excess, only to leave the dregs behind just in time for the next generation, cannot but produce a cynical generation in its wake. Somehow, Generation X got caught in between two waves of opportunity. The free money, government-subsidized life, and unprecedented economic growth on the one hand, and the high tech multinational youth-driven dot-com market on the other. X-ers grew up with all manner of child discrimination and its attendant self-hatred, anorexia, and AIDS, the fear of impending nuclear war, higher suicide rates, and serial killers. They are also marketed as a generation of risk-takers, who indulge in death-defying sports, drug culture, and lest we forget, copious amounts of alcohol. How else does one sublimate an existence forever fallen from grace?

The *x* in Generation X: the forgotten; the identical; the percentage point in statistical surveys; the exchangeable; the money-hungry middle-class; the undifferentiated. Differences between people amount to second-hand experience and a life built on a string of references to pop culture and retro fashion. A fetishization of life's little details, for example, the turn of a particular phrase. Like totally. Random classifications and hierarchies. The bigger problems are impossible to get a handle on.

Remove a variable and it hardly matters, it's all surface, and it's in how you construct the fiction that the real rises out of the mist, not in the stuff itself. That which floats above it all. It makes no difference what you say. So long as it is once removed. And sounds hip and cool. Real experience is seeing your life as a movie flashing before your very eyes.

x-treme sports

PERFORMING THE UNPERFORMABLE
AS LIFESTYLE

Adventure racing

Barefoot waterskiing

BASE jumping (a parachute jump from cliffs, skyscrapers, bridges, etc.); BASE stands for building, antenna tower, span, and earth

BMX racing

Downhill mountain biking

Elevator surfing

Hang-gliding

In-line skating

Skateboarding and snowboarding (extreme instance of)

Sandboarding

Skysurfing

Rockclimbing

Sportclimbing

Street luging

"[P]ublic opinion has reached a state in which thought inevitably becomes a commodity, and language the means of promoting that commodity.… In the enigmatic readiness of the technologically educated masses to fall under the sway of any despotism, in its self-destructive affinity to popular paranoia, and in all uncomprehended absurdity, the weakness of the modern theoretical faculty is apparent.… [T]he prime cause of the retreat from enlightenment into mythology is not to be sought so much in the nationalist, pagan and other modern mythologies manufactured precisely in order to contrive such a reversal, but in the Enlightenment itself when paralyzed by fear of the truth…." [49]

What is so appealing about X-treme sports? Proximity to death? A postmodern conception of the sublime? Crossing the threshold of gravity and matter? Attraction to the void? Or is it the presence of an "extreme gene" within the athlete that attracts them to these sports? It also seems to have something to do with the coincidence of speed, optics, and the suspension of the weight of the body. Playing in that wide or infra-thin field between ground and air, life and death. Quattrocento perspective becomes outmoded with this re-creation of the body's relations to the environment via digital technology.

The rationale behind x-treme sports, and even the TV broadcasting of such sports, seems cybernetic. The model is the virtual. The camera, taking on the point of view of the bungee jumper or the street luger, his/her body only millimetres from colliding with the asphalt at top speed, reminds one of the personalized experience adopted in video games. What was once only possible as simulated virtual experience is externalized as real. X-treme sports is inseparable from the technology of perception. The important thing after all is to be seen, and seen as if beyond the real. It approaches immortality, as the gaze of technology. The equipment and paraphernalia related to extreme sports – the cables, the headgear, etc. – come to meld with the body. The athlete becomes one with the equipment. Technology and body come together to become an *über*body of sorts. The trust put in equipment during death-defying feats is akin to trusting an extension of your very body. A prostheses. What next? Genetically-engineered robo-athletes?

What was once a product of urban youth rebellion has become a mainstream lifestyle choice for the middle classes. The first disenchantment with traditional team sports and Olympic style sporting events began in the '60s. Taking up rock climbing or hang-gliding was counter-culture for the soft grass class. Now the industry has exploded, with lots of fashionable gear and expensive equipment to choose from.

The X-sports phenomenon seems to relate to the notion of economic expenditure. An economy of excess, waste, and surplus. It relates to the idea of conspicuous consumption and ostentation. In a world of service industries where using one's muscle is pretty much a thing of the past, physical, corporeal expenditure takes on a privileged status. Back in the days of "real" tribal cultures, economic expenditure symbolized wealth through the lavishing of gifts on one's rival (e.g., the potlatches of the Northwest Coast Native communities). One gave huge feasts, offered a surplus of gifts, sacrificed their slaves, in view of "humiliating, defying, and *obligating* a rival." [50] Power structures and economies within communities were based on this form of excessive expenditure. Today, a new type of "tribalism" is manifest. But rather than expenditure being based on the accumulation of materials to be exchanged with rivals, the expenditure is internalized and invested in the body, then externalized as exhibitionist spectacle. Today, tribal markings are narcissistic rather than totemic and shared (e.g., sports logos, tattoos). The use of X-treme lingo is ubiquitous in advertising/packaging. In a world where power is represented as centreless, mercurial, and rendered inaccessible through global corporatism, X-sports prowess takes on the veneer of symbolic capital, as that x-something, exhibited and internalized by the consumers themselves, displaying the logic of marketing and consumption as a face-off with death:

"The spectre of death and a dark Greek myth may breathe some life into a struggling Alberta town. Residents of Grande Cache, stunned by the closure of the coal mine that was the community's major employer, are hoping a 125-KM extreme running race over three mountains and across a river will bring more tourists to the out-of-the-way spot. The first Canadian Death Race on Aug. 5 is tapping into the growing popularity of extreme sports and adventure racing, where competitors run, cycle, kayak, swim, and rock climb their way over incredibly difficult terrain. The town of 4,000 hopes the race – and a similar annual event for mountain bikes which will begin in September next year, will not only bring in extreme athletes, but will generate enough publicity for the town so more tourists will turn off the Yellowhead between Edmonton and Jasper. 'We've lost the mine, which was the stability landmark of the town, and the prison has downsized. We're going through a big change and need something to make up the economic difference,' [Dale] Tuck says. The Death Race moniker is tied to the Greek legend of ferryman Charon, who took souls across the river Styx to the underworld for the price of a coin placed in the mouth of the dead. Racers will be given a coin at the start and have to produce it to be ferried across the Smoky River in the middle of the race. The death theme fits in well with the on-the-edge extreme racing culture. The slogan of the race, which is open to solo athletes and relay teams, is 'no prisoners.' 'One thing I've learned from other races is that you need to have a great name,' Tuck says. They have about 100 entries so far, and he expects 300 to 500. The racers will have 24 hours to finish the course, which gains a total of 4,000 metres in elevation. The top athletes will finish in about 15 hours. The town is also putting on a festival that weekend, and is giving away $1,000 to the person who finds a gold coin after listening to clues to its location on local radio. Tuck expects it to be one of the top extreme events in the world in five or six years, and the town is working on a billet program to augment the limited number of hotel rooms as it grows. 'We want to make it something fantastic. A painful but enjoyable experience that will make them come back for more.'" [51]

Xanadu

n. Any imaginary, remote idyllic landscape or place (originally, from Shang-tu, a city in Mongolia).

A FRAGMENT

The following fragment is here published at the request of a poet of great and deserved celebrity [Lord Byron], and, as far as the Author's own opinions are concerned, rather as a psychological curiosity, than on the grounds of any supposed *poetic* merits.

In the summer of the year 1797, the Author, then in ill health, had retired to a lonely farm-house between Porlock and Linton, on the Exmoor confines of Somerset and Devonshire. In consequence of a slight indisposition, an anodyne had been prescribed, from the effects of which he fell asleep in his chair at the moment that he was reading the following sentence, or words of the same substance, in "Purchas's Pilgrimage": "Here the Khan Kubla commanded a palace to be built, and a stately garden thereunto. And thus ten miles of fertile ground were enclosed with a wall." The Author continued for about three hours in a profound sleep, at least of the external senses, during which time he has the most vivid confidence, that he could not have composed less than from two to three hundred lines; if that indeed can be called composition in which all the images rose up before him as things, with a parallel production of the correspondent expressions, without any sensation or consciousness of effort. On awaking he appeared to himself to have a distinct recollection of the whole, and taking his pen, ink, and paper, instantly and eagerly wrote down the lines that are here preserved. At this moment he was unfortunately called out by a person on business from Porlock, and detained by him above an hour, and on his return to his room, found, to his no small surprise and mortification, that though he still retained some vague and dim recollection of the general purport of the vision, yet, with the exception of some eight or ten scattered lines and images, all the rest had passed away like the images on the surface of a stream into which a stone has been cast, but, alas! Without the after restoration of the latter!

> Then all the charm
> Is broken – all that phantom world so fair
> Vanishes, and a thousand circlets spread,
> And each mis-shape[s] the other. Stay awhile,
> Poor youth! Who scarcely dar'st lift up thine eyes –
> The stream will soon renew its smoothness, soon
> The visions will return! And lo, he stays,
> And soon the fragments dim of lovely forms
> Come trembling back, unite, and now once more
> The pool becomes a mirror.
> [*The Picture; or, the Lover's Resolution*, lines 91-100]

Yet from the still surviving recollections in his mind, the Author has frequently purposed to finish for himself what had been originally, as it were, given to him. Σαμερον αδιον ασω: but the tomorrow is yet to come.

In Xanadu did Kubla Khan
A stately pleasure-dome decree:
Where Alph, the sacred river, ran
Through caverns measureless to man
Down to a sunless sea.
So twice five miles of fertile ground
With walls and towers were girdled round:
And here were gardens bright with sinuous rills
Where blossomed many an incense-bearing tree;
And here were forests ancient as the hills,

Enfolding sunny spots of greenery.
But oh! that deep romantic chasm which slanted
Down the green hill athwart a cedarn cover!
A savage place! as holy and enchanted
As e'er beneath a waning moon was haunted
By woman wailing for her demon lover!
And from this chasm, with ceaseless turmoil seething,
As if this earth in soft thick pants were breathing,
A mighty fountain momently was forced,
Amid whose swift half-intermitted burst
Huge fragments vaulted like rebounding hail,
Or chaffy grain beneath the thresher's flail:
And mid these dancing rocks at once and ever
It flung up momently the sacred river.
Five miles meandering with a mazy motion
Through wood and dale the sacred river ran,
Then reached the caverns measureless to man,
And sank in tumult to a lifeless ocean:
And mid this tumult Kubla heard from far
Ancestral voices prophesying war!
    The shadow of the dome of pleasure
    Floated midway on the waves;
    Where was heard the mingled measure
    From the fountain and the caves.

It was a miracle of rare device,
A sunny pleasure dome with caves of ice!
  A damsel with a dulcimer
  In a vision once I saw;
  It was an Abyssinian maid,
  And on her dulcimer she played,
  Singing of Mount Abora.
  Could I revive within me
  Her symphony and song,
  To such deep delight 'twould win me,
That with music loud and long,
I would build that dome in air,
That sunny dome! those caves of ice!
And all who heard should see them there,
And all should cry, Beware! Beware!
His flashing eyes, his floating hair!
Weave a circle round him thrice,
And close your eyes with holy dread,
For he on honeydew hath fed,
And drunk the milk of Paradise.

           – Samuel Taylor Coleridge
           Kubla Khan: or, a vision in a dream (1798) [52]

Coleridge's poem/dream materialized from the coincidence of two *influences*: he had been reading descriptions of Xanadu in *Purchas's Pilgimage* which drifted into his unconscious as he dozed off under the influence of a prescribed anodyne (opium). In the introductory note ("A Fragment"), the poem's origins are delineated, as are the poem's status as unfinished, lying like a ruin in a landscape, in fragments and crumbling even before construction has finished. The original poem was complete, but only in that transcendental, ephemeral state between sleep and wakefulness. The myth of the lost poem weighs heavily on our reading of what remains. The poem is almost more about what is absent than present. Or of absence as presence. It is melancholic. A colonial unconscious. A lost utopian state.

Xanadu was the summer home of the Great Khan Kublai (1215–1294). Xanadu also went by the names Shangtu, Chandu, Sandu, Luanjing, Shangji, Keminfu, Kaiping. *Chandu,* coincidentally, was also the name for smoking opium.

Kublai, the grandson of Genghis Khan, "was not only ruler of China but also supreme lord of all the individual Mongol domains, including the Persian Il-khanate, the Golden Horde of southern Russia, and the Mongolian steppes. His subjects represented the largest population thus far in history to acknowledge the sovereignty of a single man." [53] To have taken over as ruler of China was no small feat. The Chinese far outnumbered the Mongol population. In taking over China, Kublai Khan himself Sinosized much of Mongolian culture because it was easier to rule the Chinese that way. Before Genghis Khan, the Mongols had been a group of semi-nomadic tribes, with some management of herds. They had been illiterate. This changed rapidly from Genghis Khan on. Marco Polo was Kublai's agent and recorded the Mongol expansion into China and the glory of their civilization under Kublai.

Kublai's reign represented the height of Mongol power, responsible for the expansion of communications networks, the paving of roads and the renovation of the Great Canal, the patronage of art and theatre, the development of the novel, as well as the institutionalized use of paper money as the sole medium of exchange. Khublai himself was an alcoholic. He was obese, had severe gout, and his poor health no doubt affected management of his empire. He issued anti-Muslim edicts, and there was exploitation of the Khan's Chinese subjects. Today, Xanadu stands as a symbol for Mongolian independence. Because of this Chinese forces have restricted public access to Xanadu.

Coleridge's Xanadu was also inspired by the description of Manatee Springs in Southern Florida by William Bantram in his *Travels Through North & South Carolina, Georgia, East & West Florida...* (1791). Xanadu's caves of ice refer to Kashmir as described in the travel literature of Bartram, Rev. Thomas Maurice, and Maj. James Rennell. The poem also alludes to Ethiopia (Abbysinia), no doubt inspired by the writings of James Bruce, Father Jerome Lobo, and Samuel Purchas.

Xanadu embodies English Romanticism, especially under the guise of Orientalism, what Edward Said calls "a western style of dominating, restructuring, and having authority over the Orient ... a distribution of geopolitical awareness into aesthetic, scholarly, economic, sociological, historical, and philological text.... European culture gained in strength and identity by setting itself off against the Orient as a sort of surrogate and even underground self." Orientalism as a style tends toward the accumulation, misidentification, and mixing of distinct cultures into one nebulous, undifferentiated mass. Hence, the combination of distinct geographical settings in Coleridge's poem into a monolithic "mythic" land that is buried in the distant past.

Throughout the 18th century, China and Britain enjoyed relatively peaceful trade relations. Men and women of discrimination looked upon Chinese civilization with awe. Britain needed tea. At the end of the 18th century, however, around the time that Coleridge wrote this poem, there was a degradation of the Egyptian-British and Chinese-British relations in favour of growing nationalist sentiment and a growing interest in promoting Indian civilization and Sanskrit language. "Romanticism" signaled the triumph of nationalism and racist sentiment resulting from British conquest and industrial progress. A return to European and Christian ideals only further strengthened their colonial resolve. India could be exploited far more easily than China. In Britain, the European manufacture of goods displaced that of Chinese goods. Britain began to flood the Chinese market with its own Lancashire cottons.

But the real problem was the trade in opium. From 1773 on, the East India Company, property of the British, enjoyed a monopoly over opium's production. Chinese emperors tried to prohibit its sale and the presence of smoking houses, but even with Canton as the only Chinese port open for trade, the British managed to smuggle it in. As Lawrence James tells us: "The rise of the opium trade coincided with a period of Chinese decline." [54] In 1839 the First Opium War was fought against the Chinese who had been trying to protect themselves against the addiction of its people: "The need to justify these actions and exploitation [Britain's opium war], the real social breakdown in China – itself largely the result of European pressure – together with the general racism and return to Europe, were the forces that led to a transformation of the Western image of China. From being a model of rational civilization China became seen as a filthy country in which torture and corruption of all sort flourished." [55]

In contrast, India was more highly esteemed because of what colonizers rationalized as mutual Indo-European roots that both the British and Indians shared. Such Indo-European linguists as August Schleicher and Baron Christian Bunsen saw language evolving from the isolated, child-like language of Chinese, to agglutinative Turkish and Mongol to the inflected heights of Indo-European, which included the Semites and Indo-Germans. In literature and art, orientalist themes implicitly reflected the dark, effeminate, backward, and mysterious side of the Far and Middle East (Khublai Khan is portrayed as some kind of ancient out-of-control dark force hidden in a cave). Opium was a recurring orientalist and symbolist theme that evoked the sublime as well as decadence. The drug-induced dreamworld alluded to in Coleridge's orientalist landscape reflects the necessary imprisonment of the imagination within chinoiseries, no doubt a symptom of the ideological climate of denigrating "the Orient" (while in actuality the British Empire was the real dark force reeking havoc across the globe, death and exploitation by slavery, destruction of whole civilizations).

On a final note, the landscape of Xanadu is described as a fallen utopia or lost Eden full of allusions to mythic origins (gardens, fountains, Paradise, caves). It is also a sexualized landscape full of wailing, seething, panting, flailing, and pleasure. The end of the poem seems to portend imminent destruction ("Beware! Beware!" and "holy dread"). The atmosphere of ambiguity that dominates the poem's ultimate meaning seems to stem not just from the actual creation and loss of the poem, but from the very language itself which evokes as much origins and the chaos of creation, as approaching apocalypse.

KANE'S XANADU

"Allegories are, in the realm of thoughts, what ruins are in the realm of things." [56]

Orson Welles' film *Citizen Kane* is obsessed with notions of property and symbolic power. Property and power are everywhere based on the fictional, the false, the fetishized. As a child, Charles Foster Kane is bought by a rich banker, Thatcher. Thatcher had no heirs, no wife, no one to carry on his legacy. To save this legacy, to ensure its continuation, this symbolic form of survival beyond the grave, he had to create a simulated legacy, the legalized appropriation of a surrogate family, through possessing a son, a legal son. A contract is signed by Charles' mother making the ownership of his person legal. As a member of the lower class, the dispossessed, he is exchangeable, like some object on the market. He learns from a young age that life and truth can be manufactured (he becomes a newspaper tycoon) and one's true identity can be erased by the symbolic power of a fictional father. His real father was weak of character anyway, and his mother strict and puritanical.

In Charles Kane's case, the American dream of rags to riches is played out with all the material and ritual trappings accorded a moneyed status but without submission to the patriarchal symbol of power. Charles' rebellious spirit, his willingness to take risks and embark on extravagant ventures all seem to point to a crisis of symbolic investiture with regards to conservative, even anal, "old money."

Charles challenges his father's authority through acquiring a leftist newspaper business (a booming modern industry) rather than be a banker. His business expands. He enters politics. He creates an opera company. He has Xanadu built. His aspirations float from one object to another, each proving just as empty as the next. From modest means, Charles' ambitions move him to the top of the social ladder, all the while challenging his father and butting heads with other politicians. But this acquired power and status comes at a price. Although Charles' ambitions are of national proportions (like William Randolph Hearst), it could be argued that, unconsciously, he could not, in the end, truly bear the false foundations of his status. His use of power to manipulate minds, events, even the actions of his own wife, reflects the emptiness of money and power, even the tautological foundations of the law, ensured by the vicious cycle of capital itself. All speaks of the contingency of status (simply the luck of being born into money). In the end, it is the memory of his long lost childhood home that haunts him unto death; the mask of authority and power fall to the ground as some of his more "personal" but "useless" belongings rise from the mists of memory.

The film revolves around a missing centre, or a false, displaced centre: the enigmatic meaning of Kane's last dying word "Rosebud" and the relation of this name to the glass paperweight of the cabin caught in a flurry of snow. It is a rebus, a word-puzzle that must be solved before the end of the film. A maze of objects must be analyzed, pieced together in different combinations. This rebus, this x made up of Rosebud and the paperweight (the glass world of his youth frozen in time). Only the all-seeing eye of the camera makes the omniscient viewer privy to this repressed centre at the end of the film. The answer is to be found within the estate of Xanadu, Charles Foster Kane's isolated fantasy estate, that he builds after retreating from politics, to which he and Susan hide away after her attempted suicide: "a monumental setting, a mausoleum to preserve her in a living death, for his fantasy scenario." Susan, Kane's second wife, is like the Abyssinian maid in Coleridge's poem. She is forced to sing for Kane, and then is imprisoned in his pleasure dome.

Welles himself admits to the Freudian elements that structure the life of Charles' character. The log cabin within the glass ball of course refers to the pre-Oedipal time of his being bound to his mother, before he had to leave his real family's home, the log cabin. When Thatcher has Kane signed over to his care, there occurs an unnatural rupture, throwing Kane into a post-Oedipal world, not allowed the chance of crossing the threshold to "normal" maturity. In fact, the whole opening "separation" sequence feels traumatic, almost shot like a bad dream. His mother seems almost unmotherly, harsh, puritan. Charles remains "frozen, as it were, at the point of separation from his mother and, from then on, direct[s] his Oedipal aggression at his surrogate father." The impetus of his whole life, sublimated under the guise of rebellious son, newspaper tycoon, tyrannical husband, etc., seems to have frozen at the traumatic moment of his separation from his mother. Fantasies of his mother's love left unfulfilled. There is a perpetual attempt to repeat the traumatic moment of separation. Or rather, it is an attempt to freeze time at the moment *just before* this shattering experience of losing something – an ideal construct of the mother, or his only personal possession, the sled (Rosebud). His fetishistic impulse materializes as a fixation on the loss of his sled, the very sled that he used to hit his surrogate father, Thatcher, just before leaving home. The sled becomes a slippery signifier to which he returns eternally. The sled is a fetish because it is the very object of association that Charles has made unconsciously with the separation from his mother. His sled was his first possession. He never possessed his mother, nor was he ever really possessed by her. She seems emotionally frigid. Charles was a surplus mouth to feed. His father was weak of character, an alcoholic. The atmosphere of the household evokes the Depression era. The word "Rosebud," [57] by a system of displaced unconscious associations, comes to fill in for the repressed trauma: the trauma of the emptiness of family life. The trauma of losing one's most prize possession. This trauma is masked by the attempt to construct an ideal in place of this loss, the denial of never having had an ideal mother.

It would be one attempt after another to fill the void left behind by this loss of his first possession. While Thatcher tries to teach Charles Kane to think in terms of investment and money and other abstract forms of capitalism, Kane collects art objects compulsively and can never throw anything away. His need is to be surrounded by real physical objects, not abstract investments. He collects so many European art objects that he hasn't the time to uncrate them all. Xanadu is said to house enough objects to fill ten museums. While his humble beginnings are in a log cabin with just a few prized possessions, his Oedipal conflict and the return of the repressed manifest themselves symptomatically as the obsessive compulsive behaviour of collecting and hoarding. His retreat into an isolated fantasy space far away, in the middle of nowhere. His life and his massive collection of objects take on the riddled aspect of the unconscious. An attempt to return to the mother's domain through a multiplication of fetish objects. In describing some of the collection, Kane's partner Bernstein says, "Nine Venuses … twenty-six Virgins – two whole warehouses full of stuff …" evoking to what extent these female representations are empty, shell-like ideal constructions which fill up the lonely vastness of the castle, of his fractured existence. Susan herself seems to have the same status as the objects for Kane: like a mechanical toy, she repeats her operatic performances until she is driven to an act of self-destruction. Then she is kept imprisoned at Xanadu against her wishes until she finally manages to escape Kane. In sociological terms, this hoarding of art objects could be interpreted as the empty, ostentatious gesture of acquiring and displaying luxury items in the hopes of convincing himself of the legitimate foundation of his power and wealth. The display of power symbolically is just that, a front, a condition on which power is upheld and respected. All of his attempts to make good backfire in the backroom of power where a different economy takes hold.

All the objects of culture that fill up Kane's life amount to a pastiche of European refinement. Even Xanadu is not real but a pastiche of life itself. It is a place frozen in time and space, a place where Kane can live out his years in a state of deferred knowledge as to what makes him tick. In the jumbling of objects from different periods and cultures, and in the architectural mixture of the gothic, the baroque, and the classical, we sense a total denial of historical order or knowledge, a refusal to face up to anything other than the frozen moment of the traumatic separation from his childhood home.

Xanadu is also a symbol for the precarious European and American relations during World War II (going on while the film was being made). People like William Randolph Hearst (on whom the figure of Kane is supposed to be based) were against the New Deal policy and intervention in the war going on in Europe. This isolationist stance, promoted by the political right (Hearst, et al.), is symbolized by Xanadu as an isolated, decadent space that is based on European culture but refuses to acknowledge these roots (an erasure of historical memory). It was meant as an indirect critique of the corruption of the yellow press and of those opposing American intervention in favour of isolationism (epitomized by Hearst). Xanadu is at once Hearst's San Simeon and an allegory of isolationist America. Construction of the estate had not even finished yet (it was in a state of constant expansion) and already it was beginning to decay, bit by bit. It reflects the instability of America at the end of the 1930s, a state that could have paved the way for the triumph of fascism had it not been for the bombing of Pearl Harbor. America did not acknowledge its responsibility toward ending the war until the fighting began to hit too close to home. America's isolationist mentality was yet another symptom of the modern nation state. [58]

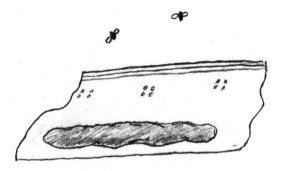

CANADA'S XANADU

"CLEAN UP OF VANCOUVER DEMANDED BY ANGRY CITIZENS,
yelled the headlines. TREES, EYESORES, MUST GO. And with that
down were coming all the horse chestnut and the maple trees
lining the beautiful leafy avenues and alleys. Bulldozers grunted
up and down the beach of English Bay, long since bereaved of the
cows ... rooting away and cleaning up the silvered driftwood that
alone to him had lent it character, though to their relief many of
the houses with rose gardens going down to the sands still stood....
But everywhere else, it seemed, the shingled houses were falling
like ninepins, each day cupolas tumbled off the poor old steamboat Gothic buildings being torn down, like the trees, to make way
for more soulless Behemoths in the shape of hideous new apartment buildings, yet more deathscapes of the future.... The fake
modern buildings going up everywhere were proving far more
deserving of literal cold-blooded condemnation than even were
those they replaced. Their roofs leaked, their staircases collapsed,
their toilets would not work. And besides a soul-destroying ugli-
ness these new buildings all had in common, both within and without, was a curious-seeming out-of-dateness. Not in the sense that
the steamboat Gothic houses could be said to be out of date. It
was that those had the aspect of potential ruins, of a sort of rubble,
even before they had been completed." [59]

Sitting here, somewhere below mile zero. A shifting between dream and reality. A wavering threshold between sea and sky. Sunday. Day zero. A threshold between weeks. Between earning and borrowing and begging. Between scrounging and sniffing. A day for retrospection and forecasting. Fewer and fewer prospects on the horizon. In the offing, a reminder of a distant land. A possible escape from this overrated Victorian pastoral.

Being away from Xanadu for a time allows one to think differently about it, more as an outsider or a tourist than a resident. The ferry rides, thumb rides, bus rides, the miles of walking to-and-fro, from one zone to another, are tedious. Xanadu creeps up on you like a Tarkovsky film gone awry, caught in slower motion. The endless panning of long stretches – Surrey, Delta, Richmond. Hours and hours of doom followed by boredom. No one speaks about anything. Bits of detritus frozen in stagnant water. The orange haze hovering just above water level. You could swear it was shot in black and white, it's so grey. Except for the dirty orange. But arriving in Xanadu after months and months of Victoria makes the trip worth the wait.

(When I'm not in that circumscribed space, how does memory speak? I have lived there, in Xanadu, off and on my entire life, but it is a time and space before my conception that interests me. Like the work of the unconscious in the "Master's bedroom.")

I imagine a burgeoning landscape full of hope and prosperity. Since its distant beginnings back in 1966, N.E. Thing Company Limited was onto something, pointing the way to the future. *Bagged Piece* was an architectural installation that Ian Baxter of N.E. Thing Co. produced as a monument to consumer society. A four-room apartment was bagged: the rooms themselves and all objects found within the rooms. The artist even bagged himself in polyethylene sheets. Plastic points to something being protected from use. Something dead. Asphyxiated. Commodities being stored for future use. Plastic is the membrane that separates ourselves from the stuff of life. It keeps things from tainting one another, from getting dirty and germy. It signals the clinical, the uncontaminated. Objects remain wrapped just like Kane's art objects remain in crates at Xanadu. When Baxter bagged this domestic space he put up an announcement: "FOR RENT – BAGGED PLACE, 4rm, self-contained furn. ste., double bed, plastic bagged, sterilized, scenic view, close to UBC, no students, non-smoker, non-drinker, no pets or children, parking in rear, open for insp. Daily except Sunday from Feb. 2. For info call 228-2759."

Then one catches a more contemporary glimpse of Xanadu, shot in colour this time. Here one finds, sporadically dotting the ever green landscape, little bags of shit. Gifts left behind by those sprightly dog-walker-cum-pooper-scoopers of the neighbourhood. They appear overnight like so many shit-packing elves working into the wee hours to bring joy to the world. Hanging by knots from chain-link fences, tucked strategically between rock and bush, mockingly set down beside the garbage can, or just plain in the middle of an intersection for gazillions of cars to run them over, until pop, the shit breaks free again!

Brilliant shiny bags glistening in the hot sun! This is perhaps a part of Xanadu that few people have had the pleasure to behold. If you're like most people and have a car, or you don't have the excuse of a dog to walk, then you probably think I'm talking shit. But no, these plastic bouquets are a daily encounter for any serious Xanadu *flâneur*.

And then there are the syringes and condoms strewn along the sidewalk. A little further down the road, the condominiums wrapped in plastic. A reminder of the sleazy community spirit, the fantastic urban planning, the superb labour standards, the unanimous feelings of social responsibility toward the average sucker. All this since Xanadu's crown jewel of an event, Expo '86. Crumbling of unions, razing of affordable housing. To make way for bagged homes for the rich. Bagged homes are a great idea when you stop to think about it. The wet climate, the economical, quaint boxes we live in. It makes sense when you think of the amount of waste one constantly needs to dispose of anyway. It's in the bag. The rest will take care or itself.

A few years back, one early morning (about two AM), a racket from down below woke the residents of Mount Pleasant Towers. The air was filled with a toxic stench. Someone had lit the blue recycling bins on fire. Brilliant! A chemical soup bubbling away down below. Blue angels melting into asphalt. A lovely apparition for a couple of glue sniffing vandals, and for an apartment complex full of sleepy white trash gazing down from their balconies.

After the decline of its wooded and stoned façade, you'd think Xanadu had a bright and shiny future in plastics. Back in the '60s, Robert Smithson had thought about covering one of the many islands off the coast of Greater Xanadu, Miami Islet, with sheets of glass. This crystalline world would slowly wear away into sand again. A study in entropics. But the project was stopped by environmentalists who had visions of gulls with cut-up bloody feet. This made way for the covering of Xanadu itself in glass, then strewn with plastic. To make a truly unified piece, a *Gesamtkunstwerk* for our time, they could commission Christo to wrap Xanadu in a giant plastic sheet (like a macrocosmic version of BC Place) so that on that one long-awaited day, when Xanadu is seismically precipitated into the ocean, it could peacefully drift off from the Pacific rim, into the porcelain bowl of eternal surf.

THE AMERICAN XANADU

Back in the '70s, a few people decided to create geodesic homes for the future. The model was the same for each one. Xanadu was a white-domed home of the future, with franchises in Kissimmee, Florida, Wisconsin Dells, Wisconsin, and Galinburg, Tennessee. These Xanadus promoted environmentally sensitive sci-fi lifestyles, in do-it-yourself structures. Xanadu's were made of wet polyurethane foam sprayed over gigantic balloons to form the frame of a low-cost, energy efficient domicile. Like living in a styrofoam cup turned upside-down. Today, the last surviving Xanadu is deserted and in an advanced state of dilapidation.

PROJECT XANADU

A hypermedia dream thought up by Ted Nelson in 1960. It was a project designed as "an initiative toward an instantaneous electronic literature; the most audacious and specific plan for knowledge, freedom, and a better world yet to come out of computerdom; the original ... hypertext system." As it happens, the World Wide Web partially realized his intentions through its interactive, global reach, but Nelson himself describes the Web as "pretty awful." The Web was not designed on the principal of a paperless system while the original Xanadu was. In fact, the Internet even imitates the look and linearity of paper on the screen. Since the beginning, Xanadu attempted to create a world of "deep electronic documents" with frictionless interconnections between sites and a solution to copyright use of material through an automatic pay for use basis. [60]

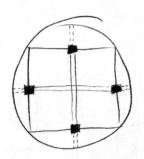

MAYAN WORLD ORDER □

- Crossroads #
- Cave openings :::
- Mountains ■
- Earth O

Xibalba

Mayan civilization can been broken down into three periods: the Early Classic (300–660 AD), Classic (600–900 AD), and Late Classic (1200 AD to European conquest). The beginning of this last period coincided with a mass exodus from larger cities to smaller towns after overpopulation (environmental degradation/depleting resources) and a massive drought caused much famine and death. Quiché was one of these new kingdoms.

The *Popol Vuh*, meaning "Council Book," is the Quiché Mayan book of creation, one of the most important texts in the native languages of the Americas. The original version, written in hieroglyphs, was destroyed by Spanish conquerors in the 16th century. The original book would have included astrological tables and ritual almanacs, similar to those found in the four only surviving Mayan hieroglyphic books (the Dresden, Paris, Madrid, and Grolier Codices). The *Popol Vuh* was recomposed by members of the three lordly lineages of Quiché who knew the creation story from memory, but they also wanted to save the crumbling remains of the *Popol Vuh* story that could still be read on the ruins of the west side of the town, the multicoloured murals found within pyramids, palaces, and courtyards. The authors transcribed the Mayan phonetically into Latin script (our alphabet). In Mayan languages, the terms for writing and painting are the same. The patron deity for both skills were twin monkey gods named One Monkey and One Artisan. A Spanish priest, Francisco

Ximenez, translated the Mayan/Latin script into Spanish between 1701 and 1703. His translations are the only surviving instances of the Quiché text. Colonization did all it could to eradicate Quiché Mayan culture through its enforcement of Western forms of expression (drama, architecture, painting, writing, etc.). Mayan style clothing was banned because of the complex messages inherent to its designs. Hundreds of hieroglyphic books were burned by missionaries. Mayan resistance continues to this day. There are over a half million Quichés today, who still live in Guatemala's highlands.

The Mayans believed that in the beginning there was a serene sea and an empty sky. From beneath the sea there rose the disc of the earth. And beneath the earth and the sea (the earth floated on the water like a turtle) there was yet another location: the underworld, Xibalba. Xibalba consisted of nine layers, as did the sky. The underworld was dry in contrast to the wet sea. In postclassical Yucatan, the souls of the dead who ended up in Xibalba suffered hunger, cold, fatigue, and extreme sadness; it was only later that the underworld was considered the site of punishment in the afterlife. The root of the word Xibalba appears to be "fright."

In Xibalba the nine Lords of the underworld were ruled by a supreme Death God: he was Zero. The Mayans came up with the concept of zero independently of all other cultures. It is related to time, to the moment of origin, but also of the end. Time (and the moment zero) was cyclical, but also linear. Every cycle would start at zero again. The reason why the Mayans had such a complicated system of calendars, for example the cycles of the Haab (260 days) and the Tzolkin (365 days), was because of a fear that time might stop in its linear configuration. By having two unsynchronized, overlapping cycles one could temporarily trump death. The end of both calendars' cycles would coincide only once every 18,980 days, every fifty-two Haab or seventy-three Tzolkin. This day was considered an evil moment at which time the Mayans had to offer up blood, virgins, freshly cut out hearts, so that the gods might revive themselves, and replenish the world after every new moment zero. Day zero was the Death God's day. Another tactic, other than sacrifice, was to find a surrogate Zero/Death God persona, and put him to ritualistic death such that Death would die and the world would be saved. The Mayans would play a ritual ball game between a player dressed as one of the hero twins, and one dressed as God Zero. The ball would symbolize a defeated king who had to be killed, and the hero twin would always outwit Zero. At other times, the loser, Zero, was sacrificed.

Above the earth, there was the cave world, in the mountains above, where the deities lived – of the wind, and the corn, of lightning, and of water and rain. On certain days of the Mayan calendar one would want to communicate with the gods, performing specific rituals, and participating in ceremonies. This was sacred activity performed in caves. Drawing and writing on the walls, burning incense, leaving offerings, or performing sacrifices. It was believed that one was in communication with the gods who lived within the bowels of the mountains. One could leave messages, food, and other luxuries. One could perform acts of excess, sacrifice, and violence, so as to ensure future peace and security. One brought gifts, but one also brought in *taankas*, illnesses, to be dispatched into the nether realm.

Caves were made of karstified rock, soluble limestone. The karst formations of the Mayan region could be divided into three areas: the mountainous highlands of Chiapas and western Guatemala, the lowlands of the Yucatan, and limestone surrounding the Mayan mountains in Belize and eastern Guatemala. Erosion of karstified rock formed into caves, which in turn housed amazing stalactite and stalagmite formations. Mayan cave paintings and hieroglyphics were also found in all of these caves. Caves were a central part of Mayan culture and belief and strangely enough Mayan civilization seems inseparable from the presence of such rock formations. Cities and towns were planned around these sites because of proximity to gods, believed to be found within the mountains and caves.

According to the Mayan belief, the Earth was mapped out as a square, with a designated centre – axis mundi. This centre is often marked by a tree or cross. The midpoints on the sides of the square world were aligned with the cardinal directions: east was red, north was white, west was black, and south was yellow. The horizon was outside the quadrilateral world, beyond its boundaries. There were in fact four horizons, each of which had a mythological mountain in its centre. Deities lived in these mountains. At the midpoint of each mountain was a cave opening marked by a "tree/cross" which had protective powers against the evil forces. The cave led to the supernaturals, to the sea, and to the underworld Xibalba beyond. A road surrounded the square, the Earth's boundary. Four roads also met in the centre from the midpoint of each side of the world, each running east/west and north/south. The roads did not stop at the world's edge, but continued beyond the edge of the world, into each cave, leading eventually into the underworld. The centre point where the roads all met was called a crossroads. There were also four other crossroads, at the points where each road met the perimeter road and continued on past the world map. One of the deities was named Ix Hol-can-be, "lady opening-at-the-four-crossroads." The Mayans used the same quadrilateral model for their towns, pyramids, temples, houses, beds, etc. They believed this four-sided model was a product of the divine.

The deities made the Earth fit for humans by creating the cycles of the sun, moon, and stars. These cycles were represented in Quiché mythology as the adventures of the ancestral creator couple, Xpiyacoc and Xmucane; their children, Hun Hunahpu/sun and Vucub Hunahpu/Venus; and their children's children, Hunahpu/sun and Xbalenque/full moon. In Yucatec Mayan, there is a similar grandparent couple known as Itzamna and Ix Chel. Their adventures relate to the four-sided surface of the Earth and its annual cycles. The midpoints on the sides of the square (at the opening of the caves) world would be aligned with the rise and set points of the sun, occurring on the solstices. The sun would emerge from and set into a cave. Many attempts were made to create humans (out of earth or wood), but the first "versions" were faulty and thus destroyed or changed into animals. The successful first humans were created from ground corn. As the chief staple of these agricultural people, corn was sacred, sent down by the gods.

The creation myths recounted in *Popol Vuh* act as an actual map of the sky. Creation is replayed cyclically year after year. The actions of heroes, gods, demi-gods, and evil spirits correspond to the movement of the celestial spheres. Creation is therefore not a single founding act, but something that must be repeated so as to continually create and maintain life.

Mayan mythology as learned through their hieroglyphics and cave painting had much to do with a very specialized organization of time and space. The spatial environment – the caves created from the erosion of limestone over the millennia – already had the imprint of the divine on them. Time was stamped on the landscape, the hidden hand of the divine. One's belief system, struggles, thoughts, and art were part and parcel of this lived experience. This land was tracked, plowed, mapped, marked, carved up. Caves hold a special place in everyday life. They were wombs of meaning, of creation, and destruction, to penetrate and to be possessed by.

Somehow the cave cult survived (albeit by a thread) the attempts at extinction by European conquest. Persistence of this cult amongst native Mesoamericans often meant torture and death by those seeking to convert them to Christianity. Colonizers brought their civilization across the ocean with them. Western art and religion carried along with it a sense of the portability of experience, not attached to place, autonomous. It marked the beginning of space-time compression where the logic was exchange value over cult value. Aura is lost, religiosity of spatial experience forfeited in the name of the power of the image, the fetishization of the object. The signifier, always on the move, shifting, exchangeable.

Sublimated sex. Sublimated violence. Blood-aphrodisiac. Meat-burnt, waste-excess, life-source for the gods. Writing on cave walls immortalized belief. The model is less history, more unconscious. Tracing and imprinting a record, a sometimes ordered, sometimes messy passage through time. It is geo-philia, reverence for the earth, but also geo-phobia. One shows reverence toward that which seems to shower fortune down on humans arbitrarily. Up one day and down the next.

Life's experience was divided up between *Kaah*, the domestic, the economic, the community, order, security, the mundane and imminent, and *K'aax*, the wilderness, chaos, danger, the mythological past, transcendence, the power of deities. The cave mouth, often symbolized in Mayan paintings and hieroglyphics as a quatre-foil, a four-sided symbol like an inflated x or cross, signified a communication point between the two worlds, the threshold between sacred and profane. [61]

epilogue

"... pure representation without metaphoric displacement, the purely reflecting kind of painting, is the first figure. In it the thing most faithfully represented is already no longer properly present.... The original possibility of the image is the supplement, which adds itself without adding anything to fill an emptiness which, within fullness, begs to be replaced. Writing as painting is thus at once the evil and the remedy within the *phainesthai* or the *eidos*. Plato already said that the art or technique (*techne*) of writing was a *pharmakon* (drug or tincture, salutary or maleficent). And the disquieting part of writing had already been experienced in its resemblance to painting. Writing is like painting, like the *zoographeme*, which is itself determined (cf. Cratylus, 430-32) within a problematic of mimesis.... Zoography has brought death. The same goes for writing.... Writing carries death. One could play on this: writing as zoography as that painting of the living which stabilizes animality, is, according to Rousseau, the writing of savages. Who are also, as we know, only hunters: men of the *zoogreia*, of the capture of the living. Writing would indeed be the pictorial representation of the hunted beast: magical capture and murder." [62]

In Plato's *Republic*, a distinction is made between the unenlightened masses and the holier-than-thou philosopher-individual in the parable of the cave. The idea of the genius, putting all into categories, necessary form, making sense of the mere appearance of things through the idea of an underlying gestalt (*eidos*). The "unenlightened" are likened to a tribe of cavemen/women who are chained in place and who take reality to be the shadows that are cast on the cave wall by a fire that flickers behind them. Some tricksters backstage. The shadows are nothing other than shadows of unknown things that lay behind their field of vision, a reality silhouetted against the wall. Or they are nothing but what stems from the viewers themselves. Their own shadow. Entertaining, really. The philosopher is he who has escaped the confines of the cave and bears witness to the true light of the sun. Socrates likened the cave to the inferior, suffering, earthbound, material existence of the body, while the life of the mind flies free to pursue higher goals. This of course smacks of s/m. It reflects the reality of Greek civilization built on the hierarchical system of slavery (made up largely of foreigners, the *xeno-* or other, but also women, etc.) versus elite, free males. Much of this attitude was inherited from Egypt (where most Greek scholars were educated) and has been perpetuated in Western civilization to this day.

This parable is quite possibly the most overused example of the distinction between truth and illusion in the Western world. The distrust of appearances has continued to haunt "thinkers" for the past two and half millennia and yet still the "masses" love to put their trust in representation. Swear by it. A system of subtle and not so subtle feints. But illusion exists. Empirically. If it has survived millions of years of adaptation, it points perhaps at an overlooked principle of survival (I am thinking here of Roger Caillois' writings on mimicry). And this is perhaps just another interpretation of what can be "truth." The honing of vision following the transition from all fours to upright made for an even more sophisticated development of mimetic constructions and enslavement. Of the necessity for master and slave. A basic symbiotic relationship found under many guises. Even big, lazy, mindless, happy slaves. And lean, keen, miserable masters. All perhaps enslaved to a more fundamental problem: that of recognition.

As far as can be told, the problem will continue to stand. Plato neglected to tell us that he dwelled in the glass tower of democracy. "They only had to look through that thin curtain of transparency and into the light...." Perhaps he was too bright for them. Replacing his own godhead with a system of smoke and mirrors.

You stand or squat or sit or lie down transfixed, a bold-faced, mindless, mesmerized x, unable to remove your eyes from the screen that, everyday, lies before you. You sleep and eat and shit and piss and think and fuck and wank and soil and wash and fix and screw up. It's a throbbing beat of off and on just so long as it keeps you from thinking of what lies behind that fire in the deeper recesses, where all suddenly drops off the face of the earth....

One of the first examples of the "birth of art" (as Georges Bataille puts it), or of signs of communication, is supposed to have come out of caves, such as those at Lascaux. According to some, these images signal the beginnings of *Man*. *Homo faber* began to construct tools out of stone, bone, wood. *Homo ludens* was the first to depart from primary survival tactics, perhaps scraping a blood-stained arrow off onto the ground or wall into as yet unknown symbols of his/her passage there. The initial soiling of the wall. Defacement as trace of a passage. Perhaps these began to evolve into a patterning of belief or relief, to be, eventually, communicated as "art." Or interpreted that way after the fact. The internal existence of this new paradigm could be seen as a gathering on the ground or an unfolding on a cave wall, as so much phantasmagoria, enacting, in the place of the real, the scenes of being, hunting, sacrifice, death, immortality.

Sometimes one accidentally gets shit on the wall. And sometimes one see signs of life in this shit, signs of God. Transmogrified shit into meat again. Looping the loop.

Some of these surviving objects and images are decidedly giving you the finger, or the thumbs up, as in the outlines of a hand on the wall, some with missing digits, made by the blowing of pigment to create a silhouette. What sign language, punishment, or initiatory rite lies behind these missing fingers? Most drawings depict animals, but sometimes there are half-animal, half-human beings (never just human). Not knowing who made them nor whom they were for. A communication with the unseen beyond, or the bowels of an animal spirit world. Hunt or be hunted. Perhaps these pigmented figments of bison and horses and deer were a way of possessing these beings before the fact or coming to terms with the anger of the dead.

The anonymous marker that simply signals that "_____ was here," in the form of an arbitrary marker of any sort, a smattering of blood, urine, or crap, then becomes a full-blown representation, a symbol of transubstantiation, filling in for the lost or coveted object itself, ready-made or christ-like (protecting and preserving), or hidden and god-like (threatening and destructive).

Our erect posture, making possible a far-sightedness culminating with the "invention" of perspective, the privileging of vertical vision over horizontal smelling. Our focus diverted to the figure standing out from the ground, sublimated from the smell of his/her ass, from the texture of your shit. This opticality reaches the zenith of the possibilities in art with pellucidity and base materiality walking hand in hand through the 20th century. All goes back to matter, phenomenology, before entering *homo ludens'* endgame. Perhaps to enter into a new stage. Known as *homo simulacrum*. A figment of ourselves. Perhaps the only decency left to scrape up and display would be to mark a public site, an act of violence traced out by this lack of choice in the matter. This impossibility of turning back. Fuck the race. Designating, I am almost gone, I no longer desire what you desire, I will no longer play the game. An attempt at salvaging a residue of historical memory. A grain of hope.

Luce Irigary postulates the cave as a womb. The gravity of the physical body, weighed down by the accidents of procreation. The cave, with all its many rooms, passages, interconnecting chambers, columns, corridors, multiple entries and dead-ends, secret crawl spaces, tombs, drawings, writings, was perhaps the first model for the book. Others like Sadie Plant see the communication system of caves as a primary model for cyberspace, an ungendered space where multiple identities, fantasy spaces, and belief systems can coexist side by side. [63] The new space of illusion where new, perhaps more egalitarian, visions of a world can be configured. Unburdened by the ostensible weighty body, in returning to the "cave," we are perhaps, once and for all, escaping the cave. Or so you'd be led to think.

postscript

X-From_:xbalanque@xyz.com Sun Dec 31 22:56:06 2000
Envelope-to: styxandstones@abc.com
From: Xbalanque <xbalanque@xyz.com>
To: <xbalanque@xyz.com>
Subject: December Calendar in Word
Date: Sun Dec 31 22:56:06
MIME-Version: 1.0
X-Priority: 3
X-MSMail-Priority: Highest
X-MimeOLE: Produced By Microsoft MimeOLE >V5.50.4133.2400

Dear S,

These days I pass the time kicking around a rubber ball in this hole in
the wall. I shouldn't though. They could get angry and drag me down
at any moment. It's happened before and I made it out alive but who
knows about next time. We like it in the cave because it's cooler than
outside under that blistering asshole of a sun. Sometimes we draw on
the wall, the ideal course taken by the ball through an imaginary game
with the enemy lords down below. We think up strategies of how to
pass the ball through openings in the sky, through secret passages to
keep the ball from landing in their court.

My twin brother, a master of the game, his name's Hunahpu. We
somehow have two fathers who were also twins and supposedly both
screwed our mother, Xquiq, giving birth to us. Another story says that

our father Hunhun-Aupu's head was torn off by the Xibalba people, hung on a cabalash tree, and inseminated Xquiq with saliva when she kissed his head. Our grandparents are the oldest in the world. Xpiyacoc is a matchmaker and Xmucane is a midwife.

It's the noise they hate down below. The thud of the ball as it hits the wall or the ground. Or our yelling back and forth as we try to perfect our game. Personally I think they're a long string of misery down below, envious of the fact that we are enjoying ourselves. Disease and torture and famine occupy their minds. If we were to continue walking down into the cave for several miles we would soon reach the mouth to Xibalba. As I said, I've only been there once. The melting faces of One Death, Seven Death, Pus Master, Jaundice Master, Trash Master, Stab Master, Bile Master. They have pits full of boiling water that fill the space with noxious vapours. Last time, they made me jump across one of the pits. I almost didn't make it. I burnt the right foot rather badly. Now I limp around a little.

One day I quietly entered the cave and discovered an old withered man with a gigantic penis playing with himself. A few moments later, from the cave's depths there appeared a woman with large breasts and ass. They began performing this ritual seesaw movement between them. Soon they were panting wildly. I watched from a short distance until their grunting reached a crescendo and then fell silent. I retreated from the cave, hid behind a tree, and waited. They did not leave the cave, so I quietly returned. They were gone. I decided to draw the scene I had witnessed on the wall so that Hunahpu would see it. He said that it was probably God K with Ix-Hol.

Tomorrow my twin brother and I have been summoned by Seven Death to return to Xibalba. They want to punish us for continuing to play ball in the cave. We have been challenged to a ball game with the lords of the underworld, our loss meaning death. I have studied the many hardships to be endured and the many hurdles we must clear to make it out alive. I am writing this because this may be the last chance I have to record my thoughts before leaving this world for good. If we win the trial, our ball game will continue indefinitely just as the stars migrate across the sky and down into the underworld, day in and day out, carrying on the task of creation, until the end of time.

Xbalanque.

Attachment converted: mojo: December.doc (WDBN/MSWD) (0001F0AC)

appendix A

In his book *Virus X*, Frank Ryan, MD, discusses not only the likelihood but the real danger of a new viral pandemic plaguing the global community, one that could potentially wipe out the human race. Viruses are constantly cropping up, mutating from other viruses, so as best to compete amidst the merciless forces of natural selection. Viral strains are constantly adapting to new ecological habitats, especially with increased circulation and migration due to aviation, and the transformation of the natural environment, and the extinction and weakening of all manner of species due to human intervention: "We have invaded every biome on earth and we continue to destroy other species so very rapidly that one eminent scientist foresees the day when no life exists on earth apart from the human monoculture and the small volume of species useful to it. An increasing multitude of disturbed viral-host symbiotic cycles are provoked into self-protective counterattacks." [64]

To be successful, Virus X would have to kill everybody it infected. To succeed in wiping us out, the virus would most likely need to be transmitted from person to person by the aerosol route, through the respiratory system. As Ryan states: "... to threaten our species ... a virus would need to combine the infectivity of influenza with the lethality of HIV-1 or Ebola Zaire." [65] Within our densely populated cities, such a virus would wipe us out in no time. The quick production and distribution of a vaccine for so many people would be next to impossible. We have all recently imagined the potential havoc that could be wreaked by bioterrorists or mad, greedy scientists who could invent and release a viral strain that could wipe out a city like Los Angeles, Washington, New York, or Dallas in one fell swoop. Some viruses that spread by air are extremely resilient, as when foot-and-mouth disease migrated to the Isle of Wight by being windblown from France, over fifty miles across the English Channel.

Viruses change through mutation and genetic reassortment and recombination. The AIDS virus is an example of a highly recombino-genic strain, thus making it difficult to vaccinate the population against it. Ryan advances the following doomsday scenario: "Had HIV-1 spread by aerosol from the beginning, we would not even have registered its existence for several years, since symptoms of first infection are mild or nonexistent ... the global village, with its closely woven nexus of great cities ... would have become one vast amplification zone.... Human immunity would have proved no defense against it. Aerosol-spread HIV-1 in about the year 1980 would have proved the ultimate doomsday singularity, the terrifying arrival of a true Virus X." [66]

appendix B

Kau neva no di yus of im tel til di butcha kot it of.
("Cow never knew the use of its tail until the butcher cut it off.")

– Jamaican proverb

Ninety percent of the world's population speaks the 100 most used languages. Six thousand languages are spoken by ten percent of the population. This ten percent of the linguistic population tends to coincide with geographic areas of extreme biodiversity. The inhabitants are indigenous peoples who still have a style of life very much in tune with the particularity of their environment. Neither the agricultural model nor the industrial model have tarnished a traditional form of communal life. Their particular language is inseparable from this way of life, language being the organizing and memorizing principle within a communication system by which knowledge is passed on about the environment and how to survive in that environment. In their book *Vanishing Voices*, Nettle and Romaine claim that "traditional knowledge tends not to be valued as a human resource unless it makes an economic contribution to the West." [67] This has become more and more apparent as scientists and corporations race to areas of extreme biodiversity in the interest of learning about the use of traditional plants and animals by indigenous peoples for healing purposes. For example, it has been learned from traditional Northwest coast native medicine that the Pacific yew yields *taxol*, a substance in the bark that is useful in the treatment of ovarian cancer. As we know, the pharmaceutical market is an extremely lucrative one in the West. With the extinction of languages there is an extinction of traditional knowledge and way of life that can no longer be retrieved. As we scramble to retrieve the dwindling verbal knowledge about our dwindling animal and plant species, we steal only a piece of the big picture-puzzle that these people have acquired, accumulated, and memorized over generations and generations.

Half of Brazil's languages are located in the remotest regions of the country (see map). The highest number of living indigenous languages are in Asia and Africa. Papua New Guinea is the most biolinguistically diverse country in the world. Over eighty percent of its land area is covered in forest and most of the terrain is mountainous. In an area about the size of France, the four million inhabitants speak 860 different languages. This bio-linguistic diversity is understandable in light of the geographical isolation and difficult access to these territories. In the case of a language like Saterfrisian, spoken by only 2,000 people in Germany, the reason for the survival of such a language is by no means clear.

Half of the world's languages have vanished in the last 500 years (at least 6,000). This rate of extinction increases rapidly as we approach the present. Ninety percent of the 250 Aboriginal languages in Australia are near extinction; only eighteen of these languages have over 500 speakers. What were once minor European languages (English, French, Portuguese, Spanish) spread to the four corners of the Earth during these five centuries of conquest. There has always been the belief that language diversity poses communication barriers that hinder economic development. This is the grand myth of colonization. It hinders whose economic development? At the height of European philology, industrialization, and scientific research, when the educated elite was attempting to discover the origin of their languages and, by extension, of their racial superiority, they were wiping out more peoples and languages (through genocide and disease) than at any other time in human history.

Languages simplify with expansion. Furthermore, language isolates (those restricted to a small region and unrelated to any other language) are grammatically complicated, rich in vocabulary specific to the given environment, and the most susceptible to the effects of lifestyle change due to globalization. What knowledge, what imagination, has been lost, is being lost? What cultural diversity exists, is gained or lost, in English, the *lingua franca par excellence*?

Some recent extinct languages:

Catawba Sioux	Red Thundercloud of South Carolina, last fluent speaker, died in 1996.
Ubykh	Tefvik Esenc of Haci Osman in the northwestern Caucasus, last fluent speaker, died in 1992 (10,000 Ubykh people were scattered across Turkey when Russia conquered the Muslim northern Caucasus – this type of genocide and diaspora continues today for the Chechen population).
Wappo	Laura Somersal from California, last speaker, died in 1990.
Manx	Ned Maddrell of Isle of Man, last fluent speaker, died in 1974.
Mbabaram	Arthur Bennett of North Queensland, Australia, last to know more than just a few words, died in 1972. [68]

appendix C

"In Iowa, there is a cow as ordinary as her name: Bessie. Only one thing distinguishes Bessie from the rest of the herd: she is about to give birth to a gaur instead of a calf.... Will she regard the ox-like Asian animal as an ugly duckling of a cow? Or a swan of a son? This is not a character out of a Hans Christian Andersen fairy tale. It's science, not fiction – a story of endangered species and reproductive technology, of human creation and, I suppose, human destruction. Bessie is the surrogate mother of the world's first cloned endangered species. The animal she is carrying was cloned from a single cell of a dead gaur and implanted by scientists from Advanced Cell Technology for a cross-species pregnancy. These researchers have called the bull-to-be 'Noah.' He is, after all, the first passenger on an ark they are building as a rescue ship from environmental catastrophe.... The gaur itself, a one-ton creature of India and South Asia, once hunted for food and sport, is now as threatened as the bamboo jungles and grasslands that were its home. What kind of a future is there with Bessie? The last bucardo mountain goat died earlier this year in Spain, but its cells were frozen. Is it truly 'extinct' or just waiting for resurrection? Can we comfort ourselves with a freezer full of cells as species disappear and the wild itself becomes extinct?" [69]

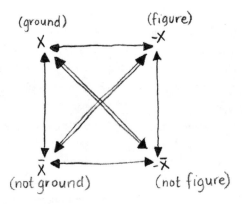

appendix D

THE CROSSING (OUT) OF FIGURE AND GROUND: KRAUSS AND THE KLEIN GROUP SQUARE GRID

"… the trauma *qua* real is … that X which forever hinders any neutral representation of external referential reality.… At the level of the gaze, the Real is not so much the invisible Beyond, eluding our gazes which can perceive only delusive appearances, but, rather, the very stain or spot which disturbs and blurs our 'direct' perception of reality – which 'bend' the direct straight line from our eyes to the perceived object." [70]

In her book, *The Optical Unconscious*, Rosalind Krauss sketches out the high modernist privileging of opticality in art, beginning with the phenomenological figure/ground distinctions, then tracing out the instances of not-figure/not-ground as they occur in 20th-century art. At first it seems that Krauss envisions modernism as a graph rather than as a history – as topography rather than narrative, as simultaneity of spatial structure rather than sequentiality of time. But while she begins with the formalist Klein Group square grid of diagonal axes (figure/ground; not figure/not ground), she ends up overlapping its formal structure with Lacan's Schema L, showing that not only do such diagrams come from a very structuralist way of thinking, but also that there lurks behind this apparently self-enclosed system of

- field of synchrony
- the visual as such
- inside
- perspectival lattice

- separation
- perception
- outside
- serial repet

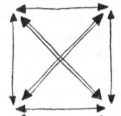

- field as figure
- retinal surface
- inscription of empirical viewer
- "belongs to me"
- part objects
- grid/matrix

- frame
- reflection
- inscription o transcendent
- castration
- inventory
- automaton
- figures of a
- gestalt

the detached visual field, a hidden world of the unconscious. A world where words and images are traced out and exist as simultaneous, but where meaning is produced through time, and where enigmatic meanings are deferred and revisited constantly through time. What Krauss unmasks is the primacy of seduction or antagonism by the "other" in the whole process/acquisition of perception and desire. "No figure, no ground" and by extension, "no other, no ego." In high modernist art the perceptual, empirical field is rejected to make way for a new frame – that of the visual field as structure. It is "the matrix of an absolute simultaneity." The cancelled perceptual field, however, is simply repressed, and therefore, preserved.

The modernist open grid, like the "democratic" architectural glass curtain wall, provides only a veneer of transparent meaning. A hidden ideology looms, repressed, an optical unconscious that is caught in obsessive repetition of desire and denial, the dynamic relationship + and -, not + and not -. Krauss explains:

> "The advantage of the graph as a picture of modernism and its visualist logic is that it is perfect. Both a perfect descriptor and a perfect patsy. Its frame which is a frame of exclusions is oh so easy to read as an ideological closure. Nothing enters from the outside, there where the political, the economic, the social, foregather. But neither does anything rise up into the graph from below. Its transparency, the logic of its relations, creates a pellucid field, all surface and no depths. The problem … will be to show that the depths are there, to show that the graph's transparency is only seeming: that it masks what is beneath it, or to use a stronger term, represses it. The relation between the L Schema and the Klein Group could configure this repression. Not because the L Schema shows an elsewhere, an 'outside' of the system. But because it shows the repressive logic of the system, its genius of repression." [71]

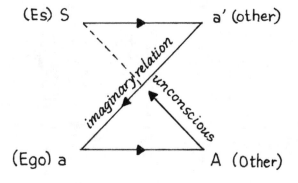

Within such a transparent system, the observer is captive to the spectacle at hand. The overlaying of the visual field onto the perceptual field is seen as objective, neutral. The structuralist graph is a self-contained space, but rather than simply representing a neutral relationship, it hides within its very logic, the primary grains of ideology and repressed thought (cf. Zizek's quotation cited above). Thanks to life's many accidents and contingencies, we are often witness or subject to the surfacing of repressed thought which disrupts the false neutrality and objectivity of perception. The veneer can be pulled away, revealing the "real" that lies hidden "behind" consciousness. The perpetual "presentness of grace" that all ahistorical autonomous fields (such as the Klein group graph) share are utopian. Always constructed at someone else's expense.

The optical utopia (as self-sufficient system) is a return to a mythic, primordial time, when a primary matrix was just beginning to turn, as the sea and the sky were separating as horizon line. Soon the black dot of a ship appears right at the vanishing point of perspective, the necessary figure to colonize an "uncharted" ground. Of violence between subject and other, and variations upon this theme. Without the knowledge of historical memory. Modernism's logic (the positivist investiture in bourgeois subjectivity) rationalizes the perpetuation of violence toward the other. It erases history in its obsession with a perpetual present. The dissolution of the logic of this graph in postmodernist paradigms highlights the need to restructure the ego formation in its relation to what could be classified as a phantasmagorical other.

That which lies beneath *objet petit a* – the black hole of the Real.

supplement

As he would read or write he would often find himself waiting, as if for the light to change at an intersection, after every x.

"For Fritz, when he was writing, the lines meant roads and the letters ride on motor-bicycles – on the pen – upon them. For instance, 'i' and 'e' ride together on a motor-bicycle that is usually driven by the 'i' and they love one another with a tenderness quite unknown in the real world. Because they always ride with one another they become so alike that there is hardly any difference between them, for the beginning and the end – he was talking of the small Latin alphabet – of 'i' and 'e' are the same, only in the middle the 'i' has a little stroke and the 'e' has a little hole. Concerning the Gothic letters 'i' and 'e', he explained that they also ride on a motor-bicycle, and that it is only a difference like another make of bicycle that the 'e' has a little box instead of hole in the Latin 'e'. The 'i's are skillful, distinguished and clever, have many pointed weapons, and live in caves, between which, however there are also mountains, gardens and harbours. They represent the penis, and their path coitus. On the other hand, the 'l's are represented as stupid, clumsy, lazy, and dirty. They live in caves under the earth. In 'L'-town dirt and paper gather in the streets, in the little 'filthy' houses they mix with water a dyestuff bought in 'I'land and drink and sell this as wine. They cannot walk properly and cannot dig because they hold the spade upside down, etc. It became evident that the l's represented faeces. [I]nstead of the double 's', he always wrote only one, until a phantasy afforded the explanation and solution of this inhibition. The one 's' was himself, the other his father. They were to embark together on a motor-boat, for the pen was also a boat, the copy-book a lake. The 's' that was himself got into the boat that belonged to the other 's' and sailed away in it quickly upon the lake. This was the reason why he did not write the two 's's' together. His frequent use of ordinary 's' in place of a long one proved to be determined by the fact that the part of the long 's' that was thus left out was for him as though one were to take away a person's nose." [72]

addendum

"It is part of the definition of status functions that the function cannot be performed solely in virtue of the physical features of the object that has the status function. The knife and the chair can perform their respective physical functions just in virtue of their physics, but the person or the piece of paper cannot perform the status functions of president or money just in virtue of the physics of the human body or the paper. Status functions can be performed only in virtue of the collective acceptance or recognition of something as having that function. But if that is so, then the agents involved in the collective acceptance or recognition must have some way to represent to themselves the fact that the object has the status function. Why? Because there is no way to read off the status function Y just from the physics of the X. For knives and chairs it is built into the physics, but for money and presidents, there is nothing there to the object X except its features as an object of the X sort. The only way to get to the Y status function is to represent the X object as having that status. Typically we represent the status function with words. We have to be able to think, 'This is money,' or, 'He is the president.'" [73]

afterword

An integral part of what we understand as the "book" is the "binding effect" of its material (pages/cover) and formal structure. If the binding of meaning in this book seems rather loose to the reader, this is an attempt, on my part, to allow the many accidents of meaning to emerge between the disparate subjects covered here. It provides space for the reader to intervene with their own connections and additions to the text, their own translation of an "enigmatic signifier" (see translator's preface). If the reader finds descriptions and terminology obscure or elliptical, this is also part of the unbinding of meaning that I intended – the wish not to be exhaustive and demagogic in view of complementing the open-ended nature of X.

This book is also a reflection on the continuous "afterwardsness" that follows us through life, what Freud and Lacan would call *Nachtra-glichkeit*, the restructuring of a past (so-called primal) event, over and over again, as the subject restructures itself at various turning-points in life. The past event was (is) a troublesome, even traumatic point, in the development of the individual. It calls for continuous reinterpretation of events. This activates a discontinuity of experience, creating a rupture in consciousness. The past haunting the present and future, and vice versa retroactively. A good analogy would be the faint trace of obscured/censored words within a palimpsest, within the continual re-writing of history.

There is no beginning and no end. No linearity to follow, unimpeded.

Only deferred thought and action. Taken up and abandoned. Taken up, sorted through, and then forgotten. The process is continuous. Always a next step to take in trying to make sense of the eternal return. Usually one puts this thought (the past event) off continuously. One encounters internal enigmas that seem to materialize out of thin air. Every once in a while a flash of meaning emerges within liminal states – between sleep and wakefulness, during intoxication, while mindlessly riding the bus, hearing a particular word. The moment of seduction or trauma, repressed and dormant, raises its head when we least expect it, and causes us to question the very sense of stability that we have attempted to provide for ourselves in our every performance. Prescribed behaviour suddenly appears false. Social positions and titles inherited, or acquired through great personal sacrifice, resound hollowly. The language we use, the roles we take on, the people we recognize or adore, or those we put down and chastise, all conventions and habits are subject to a binding apparatus regulating this system as such. Hence, the importance of "unbinding" within this book. Being attentive to the deferred, repressed element (*Nachtraglichkeit*), can provide another means of understanding how desire and ideology insinuate themselves into the subject during its formative years, perpetuating these dominating structures that bind life. The *Nachtraglichkeit* disrupts the logic of a closed, normative system. Blasting it wide open. What occurs on the level of the individual finds its counterpart in the social. There is something redemptive about the unconscious' workings, in the possibility of restructuring the individual and the social through the rupturing of consciousness.

notes

1 Jacques Derrida, *Of Grammatology*, Baltimore, Maryland: Johns Hopkins University Press, 1976, 430. Used with permission of the publisher.

2 All three entries from the *American Heritage Dictionary*, Boston: Houghton Mifflin Company, 1976.

3 John Man, *Alpha Beta*, London: Headline Book Publishing, 2000, 86. Used with permission of the publisher.

4 *Ibid*, 203-204.

5 *American Heritage Dictionary*, Boston: Houghton Mifflin Company, 1976, 1479; *The Compact Edition of the Oxford English Dictionary*, Oxford University Press, 1987, 3846.

6 The last paragraph was inspired by an article by Jim Meek: "Signing off," *The Guardian Weekly*, September 21–27, 2000, 20.

7 *Dictionary of Abbreviations*, New York: Oxford University Press, 1992; Oxford English Dictionary.

8 Michel Foucault, *The Order of Things*, New York: Vintage, 1973, 26. Used with permission of the publisher.

9 *Ibid*, 116.

10 Ambrose Bierce, *The Devil's Dictionary*, New York: Dover, 1962, 143.

11 Rosalind Krauss, *The Optical Unconscious*, Cambridge: MIT Press, 1993 218-220. Used with permission of the publisher.

12 Don Dellilo, *Underworld*, New York: Scribner, 1997.

13 Naomi Klein, *No Logo*, Knopf: 1999, 23.

14 Julian Stallabrass, *Gargantua: Manufactured Mass Culture*, London: Verso, 1996, 140.

15 Sources for definitions from Michael Eric Dyson, *Making Malcolm: The Myth and Meaning of Malcolm X*, New York: Oxford University Press, 1995; *Oxford English Dictionary*; *Encyclopaedia Britannica*; Constance Hale & Jessie Scanlon, *Wired Style*, New York: Broadway Books, 1999, 176-177; Misha Glenny, *The Balkans: 1804–1999: Nationalism, War, and the Great Powers*, London: Granta, 2000.

16 Jacques Lacan, *Ecrits: A Selection*, New York/London: W.W. Norton & Co., 1977, 148. Text modified so as to replace instances of *he/his* in reference to the subject, with the neutral *it/its*.

17 Jacques Derrida, *Of Grammatology*, 1967, 68-69. Used with permission of the publisher.

18 *Ibid*, 108.

19 This subtitle refers to Roland Barthes' book *Image, Music, Text*. The reference is important in terms of his theorization of a "third meaning" or obtuse meaning – the allegorical function of a recontextualized, isolated, frozen moment (e.g., film still), in terms of getting at new "flashes" of meaning within textual, aural, and visual representation. In photography, Barthes calls this the *punctum*, the one indefinable element of a photograph that reels you in, that mesmerizes you, that without which the photograph would lose its power to convey a more poignant meaning, about death, loss, absence. It approaches the *Nachtraglichkeit*, the return of the repressed, that element from the real that comes back to haunt us out of the blue, amidst the day-to-day normalcy of life.

20 References to these new wave/pop/punk bands from *The Virgin Illustrated Encyclopaedia of Rock*, London: Virgin, 1998; Colin Larkin, *Virgin Encyclopaedia of 80s Music*, London: Virgin, 1997.

21 *The New Encyclopaedia Britannica*, Chicago: Encyclopaedia Britannica, 1995, 33.

22 K. Robert Schwartz, *Minimalists*, London: Phaidon, 1996, 33.

23 Giogio Verzotti, "Openings: Sislej Xhafa" in *Artforum*, May 2001, 166-167.

24 Simon Leung; Janet Kaplan, "Pseudo-Languages: A Conversation with Wenda Gu, Xu Bing, and Johathan Hay, *Art Journal*, Fall 1999, 86-99.

25 Quoted in Vera Frenkel, *Lies and Truths*, Vancouver Art Gallery, 1978, 9, but originally from *The Big Book* (Art Gallery, Stratford, 1976). Used with permission of Gallery Stratford.

26 Lisa Robertson, *Xeclogue*, Vancouver: New Star Books, 1999 (How Pastoral A Prologue). Used with permission of the publisher.

27 bp nichol, *Gift: the Martyrology book(s) 7 &*, Toronto: Coach House Press, 1990.

28 Sources of definitions: *Oxford English Dictionary*; *New Penguin Dictionary (2000)*; *American Heritage Dictionary*.

29 Definitions from *Encyclopaedia Britannica* (1992); Anthony Traill, *Phonetic and Phonological Studies of the !Xoo Bushman*, Hamburg: Helmut Buske Verlag, 1985; Andrea Stone, *Images from the Underworld*, Austin: University of Texas Press, 1995; Charles Russell, *Encyclopedia of Ancient Deities*, Jefferson, NC/London: McFarland & Co., 2000.

30 Marcel Cohen quoted in *Of Grammatology*, 87.

31 Robert Bringhurst, *A Story as Sharp as a Knife*, Vancouver/Toronto: Douglas & McIntyre, 1999, 416.

32 Anthony Traill, *Phonetic and Phonological Studies of the !Xoo Bushman*, Hamburg: Helmut Buske Verlag, 1985.

33 H.F. Nater, *Stem list of the Bella Coola Language*, Lisse: Peter de Ridder Press, 1977.

34 John R. Swanton, *The Haida Indian Language*, Seattle: The Shorey Book Store, 1971; Bringhurst, *A Story as Sharp as a Knife*, 1999.

35 Cecilia Vicuna, "Five Notebooks for Exit Art" in *Poems for the Millennium*, Berkeley, Los Angeles/London: University of California Press, 1995, 794.

36 Martin Bernal, *Black Athena*, New Jersey: Rutgers University Press, 1987, 2. Used with permission of the publisher.

37 *Encyclopaedia Britannica*, 1992.

38   Transcription from *Malcolm X's last speeches* (video recording).

39   Adam Hochschild, *King Leopold's Ghost*, Boston: Houghton Mifflin, 1998, 71-72. Used with permission of the publisher.

40   Karl Marx, *Capital, vol.* 1, London: Penguin, 1990, 163-164.

41   Gilles Deleuze, *Coldness and Cruelty*, New York: Zone Books, 1991, 82-83. Used with permission of the publisher.

42   Lynn Hunt, ed., *The Invention of Pornography: Obscenity and the Origins of Modernity, 1500–1800*, New York: Zone Books, 1993.

43   *Violent Silence*, The Georges Bataille Event, 1984, 19.

44   Matt Ridley, *Genome*, New York: Perennial, 1999, 116.

45   *Ibid*, 117-118.

46   David Lavery, Angela Hague, & Maria Cartwright, *"Deny all Knowledge": Reading The X-Files.* Syracuse, NY: Syracuse University Press, 1996.

47   Richard Reynolds, *Super Heroes*, Great Britain: B.T. Batsford Ltd., 1992.

48   Douglas Coupland, *Generation X*, New York: St. Martin's Press, 1991, 56-58. Used with permission of the author.

49   Theodor Adorno & Max Horkheimer, *The Dialectic of Enlightenment*, New York: Continuum, 1993, xiii-xiv.

50   Fred Botting & Scott Wilson, eds., *The Bataille Reader*, Oxford, UK: Blackwell Publishers, 1997, 172.

51   Dave Finlayson, "Death Race can help town to live," *Vancouver Sun*, Saturday July 22, 2000, B7.

52   Samuel Taylor Coleridge, *The Complete Poetical Works.* Oxford: Clarendon Press, 1912.

53   Caroline Alexander, *The Way to Xanadu*, New York: Knopf, 1994.

54   Lawrence James, *The Rise and Fall of the British Empire*, London: Abacus, 2000, 235.

55   *Black Athena,* 238.

56   Walter Benjamin, *The Origin of German Tragic Drama*, London: NLB, 1977, 178.

57 "... the emblematic word 'Rosebud' in Citizen Kane refers not to the boy's shed of the William Randolph Hearst character but to Hearst's actual name of endearment for the clitoris of his mistress Marion Davies." (Gore Vidal, *A View From the Diners Club*, London: Andre Deutsch, 1991, ix).

58 Laura Mulvey, *Citizen Kane*, London: British Film Institute, 1992, 9.

59 Malcolm Lowry, *October Ferry to Gabriola*, Vancouver: Douglas & McIntyre, 1988, 176-177.

60 Constance Hale & Jessie Scanlon, *Wired Style*, New York: Broadway Books, 1999, 177.

61 *Popol Vuh* (translated by Dennis Tedlock), New York: Simon & Schuster (Touchstone), 1996.

62 *Of Grammatology*, 292.

63 Sadie Plant, *Zeros + Ones: Digital Women + the New Technology*, New York: Doubleday, 1997.

64 Frank Ryan, *Virus X: tracking the new killer plagues*, Boston: Little, Brown, 1997, 375. Used with permission of the publisher.

65 *Ibid*, 369.

66 *Ibid*, 375.

67 Daniel Nettle & Suzanne Romaine, *Vanishing Voices*, New York: Oxford University Press, 2000, 16.

68 *Ibid*.

69 Ellen Goodman, "Using Bessie to do what comes unnaturally," *Guardian Weekly*, Oct. 19–25, 2000, 32.

70 Slavoj Zizek, *The Plague of Fantasies*, London: Verso, 1997, 214.

71 Krauss, *The Optical Unconscious*, 1993, 25-27.

72 Melanie Klein, *Contributions to Psychoanalysis 1921–1945*, London: Hogarth Press, 1950, 73-74.

73 John Searle, *Mind, Language, and Society*, New York: Basic Books, 1998, 154. Used with permission of the publisher.

index

The *Index auctorum et librorum prohibitorum* (Index of prohibited authors and books) was the first official list of censored books based on the prohibition of heretical, amoral, or obscene thought. In 1557, under the direction of Pope Paul IV, the first Index was published, later to be known as the Pauline Index. The first Index contained forty-two titles. Printers were not allowed to publish books without official permission from church censors. In 1562, the Council of Trent was deeply divided over the Index because of its excessive restrictions. A new index was printed, the Tridentine Index, and its rules became the basis of all subsequent indexes, up until the Index's suppression in 1966. The 32nd edition, printed in 1948, contained 4,000 titles.

Some authors/works found in the index:

Rabelais	1559	Complete works
Giovanni Boccaccio	1559	*The Decameron*
Ovid	1564	*The Art of Love*
Thomas Hobbes	1649	Complete works
Rene Descartes	1663	Complete works
Francis Bacon	1668	*The Arrangement and General Survey of Knowledge*
Montaigne	1676	*Les Essais*

Benedict Spinoza 1690 All posthumous work

John Milton 1694 *The State Papers*

John Locke 1734 *Essay Concerning Human Understanding*

Emanuel Swedenborg 1738 *The Principia*

Daniel Defoe 1743 *History of the Devil; Moll Flanders*

Samuel Richardson 1744 *Pamela*

John Cleland 1749 *Fanny Hill, or Memoirs of a Woman of Pleasure*

David Hume 1761 Complete works

Jean-Jacques Rousseau 1762 *The Social Contract; Confessions*

Edward Gibbon 1783 *Decline & Fall of the Roman Empire*

Blaise Pascal 1789 *The Provincial Papers*

Marquis de Sade 1801 Complete works

Voltaire 1806 *Candide*

Immanuel Kant 1827 *The Critique of Pure Reason*

Stendhal 1828 *The Red and the Black*

Giovanni Casanova 1834 *Memoirs*

Gustave Flaubert 1864 *Madame Bovary; Salammbo*

Ernest Renan 1889 *Vie de Jesus*

Emile Zola 1894 Complete works

Henri Bergson 1914 *Creative Evolution*

Anatole France 1922 Complete works

Jean-Paul Sartre 1948 Complete works

Albert Morovia 1952 *Woman of Rome*

credits

Efforts have been made to locate copyright holders of source material wherever possible. The publisher welcomes hearing from any copyright holders of material used in this book who have not been contacted.

acknowledgments

This book would be nothing without the knowledge, advice, support, and friendship, both past and present, of Graham Meisner, Lorna Brown, Ken Lum, Michael Turner, Murray Johnston, Brian Lam, Blaine Kyllo, Kathleen Ritter, Jeremy Todd, Natashia McHardy, Amy Pederson, Erika Geske, Bob Tombs, Shelly Rahme, Heidi and Arno Willkomm, Fernand Daigle, Gu Xiong, Jacques, Michelyne, and Alain Roy, as well as all the second-hand experience I have indirectly acquired through the many authors cited here. Much thanks to Dean Allen for typographic design. The unconscious influences I might have acquired from people I have known are too numerous and are impossible to recall, but please be so kind as to realize that you too are included in this list.